The Psychology
of Love

by

SAMUEL KAHN

This edition published by arrangement
with Philosophical Library.

Introduction

by

Harry L. Goldwag, Cp., Par. D.
Professor of Materia Medica
Long Island University

My esteemed friend Dr. Samuel Kahn has asked me to write an introduction to this book. I gladly accept this invitation with a keen sense of respect for his knowledge and research in the field of psychiatry and psychoanalysis.

I believe this book is exhaustive and covers most phases of love problems. While it explains the basic principles of love and how this would be handled in a general way, it goes one step further in that it presents the simple principles of understanding of those in love in a kindly, courteous, humane manner, one that is appealing and reasonable to most people.

These problems are handled by Dr. Kahn from a psychological standpoint. I would like to inject a thought from the chemical viewpoint, and while I do not suggest that love problems be handled as coldly as a chemical reaction, we must, however, consider that such reactions do take place in the body.

No new evidence is necessary to recognize the fact that the human body constantly undergoes chemical changes. We must also bear in mind that the nucleus of the cell of the body is surrounded by rings of positive and negative electric charges. We also learn from the physicist that the earth and everything in it is in constant motion.

It is obvious all around us that such chemical changes and motion are in evidence, e.g., the rusting of iron in damp places. The human body is in constant motion molecularly and undergoing chemical changes inside and out. Increased emotions such as gladness, hilarity, happiness, joy, pleasure, etc., therefore increase the chemistry in the body, whether outward manifestations are evidenced or not. By the same token, sadness, grief, depression and downheartedness will retard activity, thereby decreasing, modifying, changing or interfering with the normal chemical reactions. Chemical examinations in each of the above instances will differ proportionately according to the increase or decrease of the emotional activity. A degenerative process may even take place.

A friend of mine called my attention to the following story, which is true to life:

"A man loved his wife dearly. Every time he would see or pass her, he would kiss her, pinch or just touch her and be thrilled, but she could not reciprocate. He asked her why she did not manifest the same affection toward him, and she replied innocently: 'Maybe your chemistry doesn't match mine.' Now, every time he sees her, he wants to know whether she has brought up her oxygen or nitrogen content."

This brings us to a very important point which may explain many phases of the phenomena in life. In nature, many substances have a natural attraction to each other, such as metallic substances, earth, wood, rock, minerals, etc. Such attractions occur when these substances reach the same vibratory rate. Everything is in motion and reaches a vibration rate at some time or other, to synchronize with other substances of the same vibratory rate. They are then attracted to each other much the same as the magnet attracts iron. We must remember that the magnet does not attract all metals.

Two or more chemicals may require their vibratory rates (surface tension) to cause certain reactions. The flesh (human body) will act similarly and manifest itself through

6

interpreted sensations. These sensations may be pleasant or unpleasant. However, in each instance the chemistry (vibratory rate) may be increased or decreased by suggestion or emotions (gladness, depression or sadness). Lovers may not realize that suggestion which has increased a polarity, or attraction to each other, is very much like particles of matter or chemicals (chemical affinity), which is similar to laws in chemistry. In love there is an interchanging of cells or their chemicals. Again, these reactions may be increased or decreased in individual cases according to excitement, love, hostility, hatred, fear or grief—if distrust or suspicion (normal or abnormal) is involved. Body cells which function normally, as in happiness, will function oppositely in grief. There is evidence that a tear drop, analyzed chemically, may disclose whether it is a tear of joy or one of grief.

Certain chemical reactions will take place in opposite sexes in the human body when affected by the use of perfume (pleasant-smelling), a pleasant human body odor, or a bad-smelling perfume, or bad body odor. Insects are attracted to certain flowers by their odor and thrive. The sound of a good or bad speaking voice, the features of a beautiful or well-defined face, a well-shaped body or the reverse, the clothing, hair, skin, the attainment of success in arts, music, business or profession, are all associated with chemical changes in the body. Holding hands, rubbing noses, hugging each other, holding each other around the waist, or kissing—will affect the chemistry of each individual body by increased vibrations, etc. Similar reactions, but perhaps to a lesser degree, could be manifested in other living animals. The reaction is similar to the state of vibration brought about by the attraction of a piece of iron to a steel magnet. There is an attraction that exists between almost all matter, positively or negatively.

Intelligent men and women may not wish to marry each other simply because they are, or are not, properly drawn to each other. It seems to me that the union of souls should begin with a marked respect and tolerance for one

7

another, with chemical changes in the body and with vibratory changes and magnetic-like attractions. There is no doubt that the thrill of a kiss has its origin in subconscious associations. A male kissing his daughter, wife, mother, son, sweetheart, sister, aunt, uncle or grandfather, will not have the same feelings and chemical changes. A female kissing her husband, father, grandfather, son, daughter, aunt or uncle, will differ chemically and otherwise. The rise or fall of vibrations in each individual being kissed will be proportionate to the past experiences and the attractions for one another.

This subject is timely and of great importance, especially in these war-torn, hate-one-another days. Dr. Kahn's understanding of humans and their peculiarities is clearly manifested in this book by the manner in which he handles this delicate subject. Between the lines one can detect the fact that Dr. Kahn was psychoanalyzed and that he is a close student of the late Sigmund Freud and others.

To be able to love, be loved, understand love and reflect love is synonymous with humaneness, kindness, health and happiness. These cause pleasant reactions, increase the vibratory rates and attract to us those humans with whom we want to, or must, live together as happily as possible.

TABLE OF CONTENTS

Introduction 5

Preface 11

I   WHAT IS LOVE? 15

II   REASONS FOR FALLING IN LOVE........... 26

III   TRUTH IN LOVE 28

IV   LOVE VIBRATIONS AND COMMANDMENTS.... 30

V   TEN COMMANDMENTS FOR HOLDING THE
    LOVE OF A WOMAN 32

VI   TWELVE "DON'TS" FOR HOLDING THE
    LOVE OF A MAN 33

VII   "THE UNLUCKY EIGHTEEN" 34

VIII   MARRIAGE BUREAUS 36

IX   ABILITIES AND CAPACITIES FOR LOVE...... 38

X   THE USE OF POSITIVE AND NEGATIVE
    SUGGESTION 41

XI   HARMONY AND DOMINEERING 45

XII   IMPORTANT MARITAL PROBLEMS WITH
    QUESTIONS AND THEIR ANSWERS........ 49

XIII   WHY MEN BECOME PROMISCUOUS........ 64

XIV   WHY WOMEN BECOME PROMISCUOUS....... 66

XV   BAD HABITS 68

TABLE OF CONTENTS—Cont'd

XVI   JEALOUSY 71

XVII   THE TECHNIQUE OF WITHDRAWING FROM
A LOVE AFFAIR 73

XVIII   SEX IN THE UNMARRIED AND MARRIED...... 74

XIX   SEX DURING COURTSHIP 75

XX   SEX IN MARRIAGE 77

XXI   DIVORCE 81

XXII   HINTS ON GETTING ALONG.............. 85

XXIII   CONCLUDING SUGGESTIONS 90

XXIV   QUESTIONS FOR STUDY AND ANSWER........ 95

Preface

Many people live as if their entire futures depend on love, while others believe emphatically that there is no such thing as love. Then there are others who have various beliefs and misbeliefs, conceptions and misconceptions, superstitions and personal ideas about love.

This book is the result of forty years' study of numerous single and married people who presented various problems having to do with love. Many of the causes and cures were suggested by the individuals themselves, their relatives and friends, or by the author. It is becoming more and more obvious that it is difficult to disassociate love and its manifestations from personality, character and neurosis.

It is easier to ask many more questions than can be properly answered; but the mere asking of a number of questions, if these are related and somewhat systematized, will help us to understand the problem of love. It is indeed a problem, even though many people tend to pooh-pooh it. In fact, it is one of the most important problems which we face. One reason why love is belittled, or sometimes laughed at, is because it is associated with foolishness, mistakes, erratic behavior, and—at times—tragedies for the couple and their children. A thorough knowledge, the proper understanding, and the ability to cope with love problems, may cause happiness for oneself and others. It may also prevent troubles and tragedies in many people's lives. It is therefore very important to study and know something about love— its causes, its manifestations, and the solutions to many of the problems it raises in so many persons' lives.

Love problems may come from relatives, from friends,

from oneself (consciously or unconsciously), from one's partner, or from one's environment. It can only be to the reader's benefit to know something about such matters and either solve, cure or prevent such problems. Many such difficulties can be easily avoided or helped, to say the least. Knowledge, and the right kind of knowledge, is power.

SAMUEL KAHN, M.D.

THE PSYCHOLOGY OF LOVE

I

What Is Love?

Love is a serious matter, as many an unhappy swain and his pensive lady have discovered. True love is both science and art. In a neurosis, can there be a normal love; and where there is too much self-love, consciously or unconsciously, as in a neurosis, can that person love someone else properly? Where there is some neurosis, it can be easily assumed that one can learn to love others even to great magnitudes. Generally speaking, women prefer to be loved, while men prefer to do the loving. Therefore, it is easier for a woman to fall in love than it is for a man. If two persons become accustomed to each other, it works both ways, namely, the desire to love and the desire to be loved are present.

Assume that there are so-called normal loves and abnormal loves. Call them normal and neurotic loves. It is natural and instinctive to have love or libidinal tendencies. Love can be described qualitatively and quantitatively, but there are no definite units of measurement, because it is a mixed emotional, physiological, and sociological attribute. It is easier to discuss love from the qualitative rather than the quantitative standpoint.

There are various conceptions of love. It will be necessary to define love in psychological, physiological and sociological terms in order to better understand this discussion. Accordingly, love can be defined as a positive emotional state existing between human beings where the emotions of one, more or less, may arouse the emotions of the other, which may be further manifested by sympathy, admiration, respect, identification and jealousy—even including rage and hatred, under certain circumstances. There is also a desire to be with the person loved, and to make sacrifices for that person whether necessary or not. It may also be relatively easy for one person to influence the glandular activities of another, together with changes in pulse rate, heart beat, digestion, and many other factors. Other influences may come from various degrees of encouragement and discouragement, with desire for excelling, admiration, attention, sympathy, approval, exhibitionism, mastery, and ownership of the other person's time, efforts, attention, sympathy, approval, work and property and a willingness to sacrifice. Based on the previously mentioned statements, manifestations may take on various outlets of so-called normal and neurotic behavior. If jealousy is extreme, one may even want the partner to fail in business, in politics, economics, or even in health—in order to be able to cope with or hold the person. This is especially true if the inferiorities of the individual are great, and strong jealousies are involved. Usually, the desire is for improvement, accomplishment and success, so that through identification, both may share the same progress.

At times, one person may be too easily influenced by the other, either in a derogatory or helpful manner. Love precipitates a hypersuggestibility in a person, and the individual usually belittles defects and magnifies good qualities. Early the emotional transference predominates, whereas later the intellectual transference may dominate. If love involves merely one of the transferences and not both, difficulties usually follow; in other words, normal love must include proper emotional and intellectual transferences.

In order to be a true lover and to be loved truly, the following questions should be asked, properly understood and answered:

    1. What is my reality and how can I best face it?

    2. How can I best solve the problems of my reality?

    3. When is the best time to go ahead and solve my problems and those of my spouse?

True love is not love if it is based on the emotions only. There must be considerable reasoning, so that intellectual transferences are also included.

Love must be free. If it is forced or interfered with by either person or by outsiders, its development may be killed. Love may be encouraged but not forced. If the loved person discourages love, there may be no love and hatred may ensue; but if the loved person encourages love, love can follow. Positive suggestion on the part of either party is helpful whereas negative suggestion is damaging. It is extremely important to remember that love must not be forced; it must be free. Although some of the causes of love are conscious, it must never be forgotten that many of the causes are unconscious and that love is the result of a combination of the two sources. It may or may not be spontaneous, but it is often developed through frequent associations if love is not forced and if there is no interference.

The home, public and private schools, and other institutions and agencies should teach love of family members, neighbors, national and racial ideals, love for work and study, as well as the love for play, the arts and education. Last but not least, all concerned should teach what love is, and how to develop and maintain it. It certainly is very important to know how to teach love and respect of man for woman. This will lead to honesty, understanding, efficiency and happiness more quickly than any other single element, ideal or interest in life. It is important to know how to obtain this knowledge and how to apply it. It may not come spontaneously. The ability to love is important knowledge, yet some cannot even discuss it. Others may know how to talk and write about it; but, relatively, only a few can actually practice it.

There are some people who would know how to love and could practice it, if only they knew about transferences and the proper time, place and person. Although there are a few who do not even want to know how to love or be loved, most people do want to love and be loved. A person who did not see love practiced in his home during his childhood, or felt the absence of love, or experienced a peculiar love, may, later on in life, practice peculiar love on others or permit others to love him or her abnormally. Therefore, it is important for parents to know how to love each other and their children, and to demonstrate it frequently. The demonstration must not be excessive, but the practice of love between parents in the presence of children, and the development of security, ethics and responsibility in children, are more or less assurances of a good love life, honesty and happiness. Although some of us grow up without being able to love, or have peculiarities with reference to love, it is very possible that as time goes on one can establish the proper understanding and practice of love and remain happy; but such individuals have handicaps, and have to put out considerable effort in order to catch up with the person who was reared in a loving, happy, ethical and honest home. It is not important to be brought up in luxury, nor does it matter much if one has been reared in the slums. It does matter, however, to have been reared in a home where the parents were congenial, did not quarrel, spent considerable time at home or other places with their children, did not belittle each other, cooperated and agreed in the presence of the children and showed by example their applications to duty, honesty, effort, system and love. Such a family will not remain poor for any prolonged period. If at all possible, children and adults should be trained to assume positive attitudes toward each other, rather than to develop negative ones.

Parents who are not neurotic will not only seek for themselves, but will also teach their children the truth about politics, business, life, science, morals, ethics, religion, music and history. They will not try to prove to their children that only their own ideas are correct, but instead will teach their children the correct ideas, or get others to do so. It is easy to tell one to be truthful and honest, but it is difficult to understand what truth and honesty are—and to know how to practice them. Prejudices, ignorance, superstition and environment make liars and fools of many. We do not like to lay aside convictions of long standing, even if false or wrong. We try to rationalize the continuation of their existence. *We do not want to see new facts, unless they tally with our past beliefs and convictions.*

When our children find out such facts they lose their respect for us, whether we recognize it or not. It is very difficult to be honest and truthful, yet the truth makes you free. This, together with honesty and love, will make you happy.

As long as a person is alive, he must continue studying. He must be a student even though he may be "three score years and ten." When a person ceases to be a student, progress ends, and he may just as well prepare for his long slumber. Therefore, become a student and remain one throughout life. After you have discovered many facts and have learned how to use these in discovering other facts, apply them properly with control. Sensible love goes hand in hand with honesty, character and happiness.

It is very wise to know history, psychology, the arts and sciences, philosophy, anthropology, commerce, medicine, theology, and many other branches of learning, but the art of getting along with yourself and your loved ones is more important. It may be necessary to have some knowledge of the previous systems mentioned before you can know how to get along with yourself and with others. Whatever you study, try to apply it in the direction of how you can get along better with yourself and with relatives and friends. Otherwise, your studying may be a waste of time.

Since psychology deals with the study of the mind and human behavior, see that you have a thorough knowledge of psychology; not only conscious psychology, but particularly unconscious psychology. Just a smattering of this knowledge is insufficient and may even be detrimental. Make psychology your hobby and know it thoroughly in all its manifestations. You will be able to apply it if you fall in love. It will help you to be a better lover, more efficient and happier. You will learn through psychology that you can predict human conduct and behavior, if you will take the time to study and apply the proper knowledge. At times your family can help or hurt you, depending on their proper knowledge.

You can help to increase or decrease your own love and the love of others. If you use positive suggestion on people and are positive with them, they will assume one attitude. If you look for faults in them and use negative suggestion, they will assume a negative attitude. Remember that a soft answer turneth away wrath.

Study your partner's mentality and reactions. Have good ideas of what your and his likes and dislikes are. Understand what precipitates reactions and cater in the direction of likes, rather than dislikes. Don't be too anxious to change the other person, but if it is necessary to change him, be sure that you do it subtly, gradually and with the proper psychological understanding. Understand the other person's viewpoints before you are convinced that yours are correct. Forgive the mistakes and errors of others and do not carry grudges. Don't throw up things to people and do not push them against the wall. You will have to learn to be tolerant, understanding, and guide your partner daily and carefully. Do not be too anxious. Watch his and your reactions and responses and be guided accordingly. Don't interfere too much and don't spy. If you find errors or mistakes, don't be too anxious to expose them. Be interested in your partner's activities and interests. You must not be too intimate with your partner, yet you must be generous, friendly, encouraging, tactful, and diplomatic. Make an angel out of your partner in your mind and in words, and continue such ideas and practices, and your partner may become an angel. Normal and successful love may then follow.

Your partner will want to love you and will want to do the right thing, if you will permit and encourage him to do so. Generally, people want to be good and want to love and be loved. Outside influences may prevent such results; but if you are strong enough and sufficiently in love, know your partner's likes and dislikes, know some of his problems and know how to cater to them, and he will love you in spite of outside influences. If you are neglectful of yourself or your partner, and if you show negative attitudes and fail to understand the likes and dislikes which belong to you and to him, then there may be errors in judgment, and outsiders will help to influence one or both of you; finally, unhappiness will result. So "know thyself" first and then "know thy partner!" Always be a student. Keep these things in mind, and you will hold your partner and maintain love and happiness. Learn how to play, how to be of service, and how to love.

If there is a proper love for a member of the opposite sex which has been existing for a considerable period, it would then be difficult to have unusual attachments for animals, particularly dogs, cats, and horses; and there will be no tendency toward the development of peculiar hobbies; nor will there be reason for excessive use of alcohol or drugs. If the libidinal energy is properly directed towards the opposite sex, there will be little energy left to be expended improperly, pathologically, or in peculiar manners. If the libido is only partially expended on a member of the opposite sex, then there will be tendencies toward peculiar likes and dislikes, peculiar hobbies, and towards various escapes in the form of too many hobbies, or too strong an attachment to certain hobbies—playing, gambling, fraternalizing—and there may be other attempts in directions demonstrating frustrations and peculiar sublimations.

Not every person can love properly. One must be normal to be able to love, and one must also have a more or less normal environment. Most of all, one must have had at least an average and decent mental hygienic background, particularly during childhood. What many call normal backgrounds during childhood are often very abnormal. Childhood experiences are strong factors in determining one's loving ability. The relationship of the child to the parents (and other members of the family, to a smaller degree) is more important for his future loving abilities than any other element in his life. It is certainly more important than one's education, religious life, finances, and other experiences and attributes of one's life. (If there are normal relationships between the parents and good relationships between the parents and children, then you have the best assurances for a happy love life so far as the individual himself is concerned.) It is not always easy to diagnose the true relationships and attitudes of the parents towards each other and the feelings and attitudes of the children toward their parents. Although some experiences may be remembered by the individual himself, they may not be properly evaluated or interpreted, or some very important experiences may have been forgotten. A good lover usually has parents who have been in love and comes from an unbroken family where the parents were honest, ethical, and loved the children properly, but not excessively or autocratically. It appears that most children consider their parents as having been honest, ethical, and fine. If they had faults, or entertained poor ethics, or committed acts of indiscretion, very often these are misinterpreted, belittled, and considered as having been unimportant. There are conscious attitudes toward one's parents as well as unconscious ones. Both are important. When an individual is excessively attached to one or both parents, or feels negative toward one or both, it is unfortunate. However, we must remember that there are always exceptions.

The movies, novels, and magazines should not influence one unduly as to what is and what is not love. Great advantage is taken of this situation by twisting and exaggerating the plot in order to make it interesting and absorbing. Very often the usual and ordinary affairs of life may not be sufficiently fascinating; therefore, authors take advantage of this situation, and twist and exaggerate plots even though they are abnormal and misleading. Love is frequently manifested differently under different circumstances. Do not identify yourself too closely, therefore, with what you see in the movies and with what you read, because you only experience some of the details, some being unrealistic and not applicable to you, while many of them are left out. Besides, your environment and circumstances are no doubt different from those in the movies and novels. Should you detect one or two similar circumstances, you may be overly influenced by these and forget that there are many other elements in your life which are quite different. Also, remember that you should not depend too much on love at first sight, or emotional love. Such circumstances are conducive to a short-lived affair. It is usually the gradually evolving and understanding love which subtly develops in you and in your partner—a sense of understanding, a blending of common interests, so that the association may remain a prolonged or permanent affair. Do not be over-enthused and say, "Well, if it only lasts a short time, that's good enough for me." And don't say, "If it lasts a short time, I will make it last a long time." Permanency is far more important than an acute, sudden love affair. A short, acute love affair does not assure a permanent one. This must be kept in mind. But if you have a good knowledge of practical psychology you may make it last a lifetime.

When love does not run smoothly, do not suddenly break away. Sometimes it is advisable to ask advice from your relatives and friends; at times it may be helpful to select one or more intelligent and experienced people to act as arbitrators, so that each can tell you the whole truth about the situation as they see it. They can explain who has defaulted, why, and what should be done in the future to prevent such difficulties. Sometimes it is advisable to go to a psychiatrist for aid. If possible and practical, it is best to consult a psychoanalyst. Once in a while a physician can be of help. As a rule physicians are not any more experienced in love and in handling love affairs than any other person. However, if a physician is respected and is understanding, as many are, he can give you valuable professional as well as non-professional advice. An honest and understanding lawyer may do the same. An educated and intelligent businessman, who is honest and experienced, may be able to give you very valuable advice, which is sometimes more helpful than the advice of a professional person. As a last resort you can consult the courts. Some people consult the courts first and professional and other people later; this is unfortunate. Many cases have been aggravated by courts and lawyers, with bad results. It is likely that some of the aggravated and puzzling cases could have been cleared up, or the relationships at least improved, had the proper sources been consulted. Very often the courts fail to cure love problems, marriage difficulties, and domestic infelicities. In some exceptional cases the courts may prove helpful, but this is rare.

Except in cases where one of the parties develops an acute emotional upset and can't reason properly, or is influenced temporarily by some troublesome person, the court may temporarily quiet the situation, and as time goes on it may be cleared up; but this is a very rare occurrence because, usually the court aggravates situations, increases hostilities, hatred, lies, distrusts and antagonisms. The court frequently assumes that because of its authority it understands situations; yet judges as a rule are not especially trained and experienced in psychology and human relations. A very few may be exceptional. Both sides in a court room frequently fabricate, exaggerate, mix up and displace matters and do not wish to reveal the actual truthful details. It is very easy to prejudice judge and jury. Although most of us like to see absolute justice prevail in all courts, there are many cases where justice is ruled out, repeatedly, because of ignorance, prejudice, misinformation, untruth and scheming lawyers, whose chief desires are to win. A psychoanalyst is not prejudiced on either side. He hears all the information and tells neither party what the other has said. Although he may hear some fabrications, he comes to know the real truth more than the individuals involved. Then he adds his knowledge and experience in psychology, both conscious and unconscious. He leads the individual to understand the conscious and unconscious, and to know not only the truth, but the whole truth—unless relatives and friends who encourage lies interfere, and then the analyst cannot know the truth. The physician, the lawyer and the others involved who may be called in on such cases may also be misled and prejudiced. Love is a complicated group of feelings, coupled with normal and abnormal emotions, which interplay between two persons and result in normal and abnormal behavior, depending upon previous experiences and the environments of these individuals.

II

Reasons for Falling in Love

Important reasons for falling in love:

1. The desire for attention and affection.
2. The desire for sexual gratification.
3. The desire for a family.
4. The desire for a home.
5. The desire for a "meal ticket."
6. Reaction to the insecurity of health, age, finances, and the fear of being a social outcast, because of late or no marriage, or the fear that relatives or friends may consider the person mentally, physically, or socially abnormal.
7. Believing one-self inferior to the other person, either socially, educationally, financially, or otherwise; (the individual believes that he is making a good catch and therefore, through auto-suggestion, talks himself into loving).
8. Having failed in love or having been disappointed, another attempt is made which sometimes is very successful and at other times unsuccessful.
9. Seeing and feeling, consciously and unconsciously, some of the traits of another loved one in this person, and hence, through identification, also loving this person.
10. By constantly socializing, one person becomes accustomed to another and finds out some valuable traits in this person which, together with various conveniences and common interests, finally develops love; perhaps a result of auto-suggestion, which revolves around the admiration of physical, mental, educational, social or economic traits, the end resulting from companionship.
11. Because of pregnancy.

12. Because of money.
13. Because of great prestige and influence.
14. Because of fears and death.
15. To get away from home.
16. To get narcotic drugs.
17. To take a chance and trusting luck.
18. Because of religion.

III
Truth in Love

Before you can truthfully love somebody else, it is necessary to love yourself honestly. If this point is neglected, the time will come when you will not only punish yourself and thus bestow suffering on yourself, but also the other person will be punished. Not only must you be convinced that you want to love this particular person and that you do love this person, but, in addition, you must understand some of the important reasons for your love for permanency.

Do not talk yourself into being in love with a person simply because you are not strong enough to get out of the situation. In order to try things out, you may use autosuggestion to convince yourself that you are in love with a person, which may lead you into telling him (or her) that you are in love with him; then, later, you may find out that it was a mistake. Don't be too anxious to commit yourself! You can associate with one or more people without committing yourself. However, frequent associations with an individual may prove that you are in love, a fact which you could not have discovered before. The probabilities are that the association helped to re-educate both of you, so that you could get a better understanding of one another's environment, of your common likes and dislikes. You might then reason your way into a future life which might be mutually beneficial. On the other hand, frequent associations may lead to the discovery that one of you is neurotic, peculiar, dishonest, incompetent, or incompatible.

It is easy to tell someone to be honest and truthful with himself and others. It is always difficult to know when someone is honest and truthful with himself and others. It may also not be so easy to face honesty and truth, even though one may know the truthful and ethical facts. To be able to recognize the truth is difficult because of one's own limited appreciation of facts, an appreciation which is often misguided by circumstances and by misrepresentation on the part of others. In short, one must know oneself first before one can know one's partner. Then it can be said that "to mine own self have I been true, in order that I can be true to my loved one!"

IV

Love Vibrations and Commandments

It is assumed by some that all matter can be expressed in terms of energy—some kind of force or vibration, or various waves of definite lengths, strengths, concentrations and frequencies. The differences between light and heat, sound and mechanical mobility, revolve around various wave elements within their vibrations and subliminal movements. The chief difference between one sound and another, or even one particular light and another, also involves similar elements. The same applies to radioactivity and television. It is believed that telepathy and spiritualism, if they exist, include such etiologies.

Similar situations apply to chemical changes, whether they are physiological, organic, or inorganic. Life and the emotions involve chemical changes and so we assume that love energy includes wave vibrations. It is speculative to assume that when the love waves of one person harmonize or synchronize in simple ratios with the vibrations of another person, there may be possibilities for successful love, and when these vibrations show disharmony, or if the waves become disharmonious, then theoretically and relatively, love is unsuccessful.

If it were possible to prove or disprove this theory by harnessing, analyzing and understanding these waves, their ratios, proportions, concentrations, etc.—either electrically or through physiological, kymographic tracings or other means—then it might be possible to scientifically prognosticate a successful love affair rather than depend on the usual trial and error method.

The next question is: "In unreciprocated cases of love, where the heart pitter-patters in one case but not in the other, what are the differences in the waves and in the vibrations, and what can be done to cause a harmonious and sympathetic change in either one or the other parties concerned?" It is easier to assume that the answer may be given in sociological, psychological, and physiological terms rather than in our speculative theories, whose units have not yet been defined or classified, either qualitatively or quantitatively.

V

Ten Commandments for Holding the Love of a Woman

1. Don't lie to her and let her catch you.
2. Don't fail to compliment her frequently.
3. Don't fail to whisper endearing things to her.
4. Don't boast about your sexual capabilities, and never mention your previous sexual experiences.
5. Don't fail, from time to time, to compare her with others—and always to her advantage.
6. Don't fail to show your consideration of her by words and deeds.
7. Don't break dates with her or fall down on your promises.
8. Don't fail to compliment her on her physical appearance and her sexual technique (if married).
9. Don't fail to show her attention and consideration in the presence of others and don't pay attention to other women in her presence.
10. Don't fail to do things for her, thereby making her dependent on you.

VI

Twelve "Don'ts" for Holding the Love of a Man

1. Don't ask personal questions.
2. Don't boast of your present or previous love affairs.
3. Don't create too much jealousy, although it might be wise to make him a little uncertain of you.
4. Don't fail to look your very best at all times, so that he will be proud of you.
5. Don't fail to make an "angel" of him, and express your love frequently.
6. Don't fail to cater to him mentally, physically and emotionally.
7. Don't fail to maintain a "give and take" policy.
8. Don't belittle his relatives and friends.
9. Don't become too intimate or spy on him.
10. Don't permit him to develop and grow, while you retrogress. Keep in step with him as he progresses.
11. Be sure not to repulse him because of odors, bad character and family members, and others—who may interfere.
12. If you must disagree, be sure that you are absolutely right (after careful investigation) and then be very tactful and very confidential.

VII

"The Unlucky Eighteen"

(Reasons for Dissension Between Sweethearts, Husbands and Wives.)

1. Promiscuity, infidelity and sexual incompatibility.
2. Ignorance, dishonesty, narrow-mindedness and taking sides of others against him.
3. Financial reverses or other serious difficulties which cannot be handled properly.
4. Interference from parents, ministers, physicians, relatives and friends, either because of ignorance, narrow-mindedness, misunderstanding, jealousy, misinformation, viciousness or lies.
5. *Marked differences* in age, financial status, religion, social standing, background, education, physique, likes and dislikes.
6. Acute differences in opinions, which were developed in the individual prior to, or since, their meeting.
7. Personality or character defects, such as serious inferiorities, superiorities, boastfulness, shyness, over-aggressiveness, selfishness, negativism, peculiar fears and superstitions, inability to love or understand the other's viewpoints, and serious difficulties arising from Oedipus and Electra complexes, and other fixations, addictions and sicknesses.
8. Professions and occupations of such natures that cause incompatibility and difficulties.
9. Excessive dependence and insufficient independence.
10. Lack of knowledge of the psychology of getting along with people.

11. Accidents which may cause mental and physical chronic illnesses.
12. Children and other relatives, especially those which present serious special problems.
13. The advancement of one, while the other retrogresses.
14. Not wanting or being unable to grow, learn and develop.
15. Unwilling to help and failing to encourage the bread-winner; demoralizing and injuring him or her—by spending or damaging the income.
16. Forcing your in-laws and other family members upon your spouse against his wishes.
17. In-laws, grandparents and others interfering and encouraging difficulties.
18. Frequent criticisms and blaming the spouse for your own faults and failings.

VIII
Marriage Bureaus

There are some marriage bureaus which are beneficial. It is very possible for a couple to meet after a correspondence which was instigated by a friendship club or a marriage bureau. A normal and fine love may develop, with a subsequent marriage. What is the difference whether one meets a person through a bureau, or by introduction through a friend, or at a social gathering? It must also be remembered that there are certain bureaus which guarantee anything and everything for a price. Then it is up to the individuals, as it is in all cases of friendship clubs, marriage bureaus, or introductions through clubs, friends, relatives, and others. This does not mean that suddenly there is developed love at first sight. But through the introduction, there is the opportunity for the two individuals to get to know each other better, and for the development of admiration, understanding and love. These bureaus can be called "Romance Institutions." Ordinarily, one does not depend on these bureaus for meeting members of the opposite sex, but there are circumstances where individuals live in small communities or where a person wants a special type of individual, whom he or she cannot find in his or her locality; therefore, his wants are described and the bureau may have a registered person who may approximate such a description. After it is followed up, sometimes the situation works out very satisfactorily.

There need be no resentments on the part of marriageable people because their grandparents, parents, or other relatives want to introduce their future partners or future prospects. This does not mean that the parents and relatives select one person and "you must fall in love and marry this person." This is an unfortunate situation because when a forced demand is made that you must love and marry "so and so," a negative attitude develops, and love is then very difficult. Nevertheless, there is no reason why you should not listen to the advice of others who are older than you, or meet one or more people through relatives and others with no prejudices, and then come to your own conclusions. It does not matter through what sources or how you meet your partner. Leave all gates open.

IX

Abilities and Capacities for Love

It can readily be acknowledged that some people have more than others and that some are vested with abilities for different degrees of love. There are some people who can only love themselves, while there are others who can love others to limited degrees or who can love only certain types of people. Children who never loved either parent seldom can love anyone else. And, if they hated both of their parents, they will probably hate humanity in general. A child who hated one of his parents, or loved only one of the parents, will have a peculiar ability to love, but may become normal if he meets an individual who is the right type of person and is able to exert the proper influence. Many people will say, or believe, that he loved one or both of his parents when the opposite was the case, and in time the hatred either was repressed and forgotten, consciously, or he got the hatred under some control, or displaced the hatred upon others.

A girl who hated her father and loved her mother may be able to love, but with difficulty. If she loved her mother and her brother, or grandfather, her possibilities of love are better. The best future for a capacity to love is one who truly loved both her father and mother about equally.

The son who hated his mother may never be able to love the opposite sex. If he loved his father or mother excessively, he may love the opposite sex, but only peculiarly or with difficulty. He may also become a homosexual, a neurotic bi-sexual, or will be maladjusted. If he really loved his father and mother equally, his future with regard to love is assured, unless he should unfortunately meet some very difficult member of the opposite sex. The fortunate situation is that even though one's background, environment, and mental hygiene are inimical to the ability to love, through the proper knowledge of unconscious psychology, psychoanalysis, and certain forms of mental re-education it is very possible that one can become a capable lover.

As a result of abnormal loves or attachments by the parents and children, there are various capacities for love and hate—some of which may be exemplified through the following: Looking for faults in the opposite sex and, when finding a small deviation, magnifying it; carrying grudges, not forgiving, making accusations of cruelty, unfaithfulness, inabilities, incapacities; "showing up" the partner, or frequently "shoving the person against the wall"; trying to get money, jewelry, property, and belongings, frequently and unreasonably, together with increasing the expense, efforts, or demanding more attention and work; making threats, abusing the courts, relatives, friends, or business associates; competing, trying to "show up" the other person; talking about the other person and endeavoring to turn children, relatives, and friends against him; bringing up repeatedly the marriage vow and various promises; refusing requests, demands, or wishes; finding various excuses for bickering, accusing the other person whether he is right or wrong; over demanding various promises, together with worldly goods, attention, and time; being extremely sensitive and over reacting to small frustrations and criticisms and excessive jealousies. These are just a few of the attitudes and behaviors which are more or less influenced by the unconscious, but may be unrecognized as such.

On the other hand there are some who permit their partners liberty and freedom and are constantly encouraging them; and instead of looking for faults and deviations, good qualities are sought out and exaggerated. There is complete cooperation and appreciation. Faults and difficulties are made little of, and the individual is protected from outsiders, even though there may be difficulties.

Excessive demands on time, attention, love, finances, and worldly goods are minimized. There is a tendency, more or less towards unburdening rather than burdening, with the maintenance of a friendly spirit toward this individual, his relatives, friends and all concerned. There is no needless arguing, but instead, a reasonable acceptance of the other's opinion. There are numerous attempts at reconciliations and explanations. There is an understanding, the desire for knowing the likes and dislikes of the other person. There are no scenes and no exposés; instead, they are prevented and friendship with pleasantness is substituted.

There are some who surrender themselves excessively to others, while there are many who are too stubborn to yield and find many excuses for rifts. It is not wise to act in such directions which will be meaningless, yet one should not submit excessively without understanding what it may lead to. Each love partner should gradually try to train the other one to a better understanding of his ideas and attitudes, so that there can be a better adaptation to the children. Both should study themselves and each other, but one must take the lead. It is wiser for the man to have the responsibilities of making a living, and for the woman to have the responsibilities of the household. The children's responsibilities should be divided. The same applies to socialization and religious activities. In cases of differences of opinion, one or more intelligent, experienced and impartial outsiders should be called in for arbitration purposes. However, this should seldom be necessary.

X

The Use of Positive and Negative Suggestion

It is often true that when you frequently tell a man what he is, so will he be if you tell it to him often enough. The same applies to a woman. The following prologue will exemplify this situation: Evelyn opens the door and lets Robert into the house, saying, "Just like you! You can't ever come home on time. I'll bet you had to take some woman to the train or see her home. While I'm here worrying and waiting for you while the food is getting cold. You will never learn. At least you could have brought me a gift as an apology. What's the use? You never were any good and you never will be. It isn't in you and it isn't in your family. I gave up hope a long time ago. I am just wasting my breath. What a fool I was to have married you. I should have known this would happen—I should have expected it—and now I'll know what to do in the future."

This man got this sort of talk regularly for long periods. One day Evelyn was going to repeat her negative suggestions and discouraging formula. She waited and waited, but Robert failed to appear. Several days later she received a letter from a lawyer, stating that she was being sued for divorce.

Across the street there lived a couple whose relations were quite different. Sylvia was reared in a home of love, culture, faith, trust, confidence and encouragement. She was also taught, academically and by example, the value of positive suggestion. When David was on his way home from work, she met him at the door. She kissed and hugged him, took his hat and coat, and accompanied him to the living room. She told him that he looked well and wanted to know if he was ready to eat his dinner or whether he wanted to wash up and relax first. While he washed, she placed the warm food on the table. She looked sweet and angelic. She did not mention, or let him know in any shape or form, that she was perturbed because of his lateness.

When David said, "Honey, I am sorry to be late," she answered, "Never mind. I don't care why you are late. It doesn't matter. If you are late, you must have a good reason for it, and if the reason is good enough for you, it is good enough for me. Go into the bathroom and wash."

This he did promptly, and after he had washed himself, she handed him his house slippers and told him that he could take his time and need not hurry.

At the dinner table, she never mentioned or hinted that she wanted to know the reason for his lateness. She changed the subject entirely and was very gay and entertaining. She didn't tell him what to eat, or how wonderful the food was, or how much he should eat. She did say that she enjoyed the dinner very much and hoped that he liked the same kind of food. She also asked him if he wanted more food, and if he had had enough. She did not ask him again.

She did not bother him with matters which would be unpleasant, nor did she fire a barrage of questions at him. She listened to his likes and his interests. She let him believe that whatever he said and did was all right, that she had all the confidence in the world in him, and that she was perfectly satisfied with his behavior. She made him believe that he was an "angel."

In the future, David began to think of himself as an "angel," and he really could not act otherwise. When a fellow worker tried to tempt him to tarry, which would cause him to be late at home, David could not and did not yield! Instead, he said, "I must be home on time"—and he was!

The moral is: DON'T USE NEGATIVE SUGGES-

TION. DON'T DISCOURAGE YOUR PARTNER. DON'T FIND FAULT. DON'T BELITTLE.

If you see negative traits, don't enlarge upon them. On the other hand, be encouraging, look for the good qualities, and cater to the likes and pleasures of the individual. Such an attitude on your part will result in a similar attitude towards you!

In other words, we can amend an old proverb: "As you do unto others, so will they do unto you!" Use positive suggestion and say to yourself, "I am a truthful and loyal lover, a dutiful husband or wife." Convince yourself that you are these things and think repeatedly about how you can make yourself worthy of being a good wife, a good husband, a good sweetheart, or a devoted mother or father and always try to do the right thing. Repeat to yourself that you are patient, and that you will guide your partner daily, if necessary, rather than argue or become irritable and angry. Talk things over rather than become disgusted or leaving things in the air. Have definite understandings and live up to them. If you are to be a loving husband, a loving wife, a loving sweetheart, make yourself worthy of it, even if you have to sacrifice daily. By so doing you will be admired by all concerned. If you think indifferently or avoid duties and responsibilities, you will find that it is usually a mistake. It is better to face most situations. Do not try to make an impression on anyone; just do the thing which will bring the most happy results.

At times, a kind and encouraging word may be far more important than being neat and well-dressed. It is advisable to use kind and encouraging words, as well as being neat and clean. Say to yourself that you are and will be encouraging and helpful. Repeating such thoughts or statements will help you put them into practice. It is important to remember that telling yourself or others that you or they have certain characteristics and traits will help not only in producing such traits but in maintaining them. An adult also responds to suggestions, just as a child does, but perhaps not to the same degree. *If Johnny is told repeatedly that he is a fine, clean, little boy and that he wants to be neat and clean and, therefore, he bathes every night, or every morning—by repeating it to him in a pleasant, understanding, and interesting tone, with a kind voice, he will carry out these suggestions.* On the other hand, if you nag Johnny, make it very unpleasant for him by telling him that he is dirty, always was, and always will be, that he is no good, and use other derogatory remarks, it will be difficult for Johnny to keep himself clean. Whether or not he may want to, the probabilities are that he would get a greater "kick" by staying dirty. These principles of positive and negative suggestion also apply to adults.

Say, "I know John will never neglect his father and mother, he always takes care of his relatives, he never neglects his family, he is a real 'he man,' he is very considerate and affectionate, it is part of his make-up." Compare these statements with the following, which repeatedly will produce the results of negative sugestion: "Tom never cared about his father or mother or his family. He is selfish. Why should he care about anyone else in his family? He never was considerate and he never will be; it just is not in him. He is no good." These suggestions, if repeated, will result in his being no good.

The moral is: if you can not use positive suggestion and auto-suggestion, don't use negative suggestion or negative auto-suggestion. If Mary bickers with her husband, don't say, "Here, you are always bickering. It looks like you could not live without bickering." It is better to say, "Well, you very seldom bicker. I know you don't mean it and in case you do, it is of no consequence. I am sure you will stop it, because this is not like you. You are too nice for that."

XI

Harmony and Domineering

Suggestions For Harmony Between Sweethearts And Marital Partners

1. Maintain honesty, truthfulness, and good character.
2. Prevent jealousies.
3. Do not belittle your partner and do not find fault.
4. Do not look for faults, but if you find them, do not magnify them. Rather, minimize them. Look for the good points and enlarge upon them. If you must correct your partner, do so in a guarded, flattering manner.
5. Do not boast or brag about yourself.
6. Do not "free associate," and tell your partner everything that is on your mind about yourself, your partner or others. Never belittle others.
7. Use positive suggestion and tell your partner that he is exactly what you want him to be. By repeatedly mentioning these things the individual will ultimately become that way.
8. If you know your partner's weaknesses and faults, do not constantly throw them up to him.
9. If you show your partner that you know his (or her) guilts, and faults, and "shove him up against the wall," you will be disliked, and your own weaknesses and faults will be constantly looked for and exaggerated.
10. "Forgive and forget!" Don't expect perfection. Remember that the more you live with a person, the more you may find out that he (or she) deviates from angelic behavior. There are no angels on earth.
11. By the constant use of good and positive suggestion,

you can make the person over, so that ultimately you will really find in him the good qualities you want to see.

12. The more emotional you are, or the more you make your partner emotional, the less reasoning there will be. By using kind and tender thinking on your part, with regard to your partner, kindness and tenderness will be returned to you. Endearing remarks (punctuated with gestures) are recommended at reasonable intervals.

13. You must love in order to get love. Then you must work to keep it. If it is worth having, it is worth working for.

14. *The more you sacrifice—for a normal person—the more he will sacrifice for you. There are some individuals who are masochistic; these people love to suffer and are happy when they make sacrifices. Do not deny them such pleasures, unless it reaches extremes.*

15. *Study your mate, discover his or her likes and dislikes, and cater to the likes, and not to the dislikes. These peculiarities may be the key to one's future happiness or unhappiness in love.*

16. Pay attention to your personal appearance. Let your mate be proud of you when you go out together, rather than be embarrassed.

17. Use endearing names, emotionally expressed, with the proper gestures. These are very helpful in giving your mate a feeling of security.

18. Make your home attractive, restful, and according to the relaxation needs of yourself and your partner. Do not be over-cautious about the handling of furniture, rugs, household articles, etc. It is the comfort and emotional security which is important in a home.

19. Modulate your voice and actions so that the impression is that of ease, relaxation and security. Yet, be kind, warm and responsive.

20. *Never evade your responsibilities or duties, or an opportunity to be helpful.*

21. *Give encouragement to your partner.*

22. *Keep informed on current events and have one or more interesting hobbies. Learn interesting and entertaining ways. Study ways and means of personal improvement.*

23. Avoid arguments, but if they should start, cut them short as soon as possible and immediately resort to honesty and logical reasoning or run out of the house. At times, it may be necessary to call in an impartial and intelligent arbitrator.

24. In serving food, always serve your mate first. The only exception is when his or your parents are present.

25. Do not pay too much attention to others—be they guests or relatives—when your mate is present.

26. Avoid unpleasant body odors or any other form of personal uncleanliness.

27. Be systematic in all your activities and assign definite responsibilities to each other.

28. *Make yourself useful and necessary to your partner.*

29. *Do not discuss your previous love affairs, or your relatives' experiences, except under exceptional circumstances.*

30. *Be psychoanalyzed and encourage your partner also to be psychoanalyzed!*

Don't be over-domineering, or permit yourself to be overdomineered. Either one of these traits or attitudes will destroy or interfere with love. It must be remembered that a small degree of dominance and aggressiveness on the part of the male is necessary, and submission to and desire for being dominated on the part of the female is helpful. It is more-or-less instinctive for the two sexes. If these traits are reversed, it is unfortunate. One must take the lead and in our civilization, it is the man. *The male who shrinks from such aggressiveness and leadership is abnormal. On the other hand, the female who is the aggressor and takes the lead has had bad mental hygiene, and is either pathological, mentally or emotionally abnormal, or is surrounded by an unhealthy environment. At times, because of the lack of efficiency on the part of the male, the female is forced to take the domineering role. This, again, is unfortunate. On the other hand, there are men who abuse the aggressive and domineering instinct, and carry it out to extremes, while some women are excessively passive, or are too submissive and are more or less over-dependent and helpless. Such extremes should also be avoided. Generally, a man prefers a woman to be somewhat dependent on him and the normal man prefers a "leaner" rather than to lean himself.*

XII

Important Marital Problems with Questions and Their Answers

1. *The Problem of the Other Man or Woman.*

The problem of the other man or the other woman is acute. If your partner does not know how to hold you, but instead drives you away, even though once there had been love, your problem is then only half solved. It may be as big a problem to know how to hold your loved one, which may depend upon what you do or what you fail to do, as well as your likes and dislikes, your stability, personality, character, outside influences and other environmental factors. If there are quarrels because of negativism, irritability, neglect, misunderstanding, a lack of psychological understanding, and many other reasons, you then leave loopholes for more difficult problems. It is very easy to see one side and not the other person's view-point. We frequently blame the other party and actually believe that the other party is at fault, when in reality we force the other person into what he does. Or we may help to shape his attitudes toward himself, or other people, and then still blame him. What caused the other person's attitude and behavior? What pushed him into it?

In order to be a good lover, one must not only be honest, educated and intelligent, but also be well-versed in the art of getting along with people and in being able to sense quickly one's likes and dislikes. Otherwise there may be the problem of the other man or the other woman. Frequently it is not merely one act or two acts of a person, but it is the

49

result of many omissions and commissions, some of which may have been forgotten but were sufficiently potent at the time to establish definite attitudes, trends and reactions. Usually, it is a combination or repetition of certain behavior and attitudes which finally "breaks the camel's back."

2. *Man's or Woman's Irritability.*

Are you a smooth individual or are you touchy, complaining and irritable about personal appearance, various foods, speech, manner, dress, housing, budgeting, socializing, relatives, opinions and many other situations? Are you easy to get along with? Do you make a "mountain out of a mole-hill?" Do you make the home inviting? Is your company pleasing, restful, relaxing, and do you establish an environment of security? Or do you keep the other person tense, fidgeting, in suspense, fearful and ready for anything which may happen? Do you smooth things over, fit in nicely, become moldable and adaptable? Or do you "blow up," nag, and become worrisome? Do you look for troubles and are you fault-finding? Do you forgive easily, or do you carry grudges, pout, and dig at the other person? These are just a few questions to which you can add many which are sufficiently suggestive to show whether a person could or should fall in love with you and "stay put," or not.

3. *How to Conduct Oneself with Relatives and Friends.*

Do you know how to conduct yourself with children, in-laws, friends, and other people? Do you tease them or do you become indifferent? Do you like to "show them up," or do you like to present to them what a "big-shot" you are, and demonstrate various exhibitionistic trends? Do you boast about yourself and your family? Do you agree with people and prove amiable or do you look for arguments? Are you genuinely helpful and friendly, or do you hide and evade questions and activities? Are you an excessive flatterer for definite purposes, or are you too honest? Do you belittle yourself and other people? Do you degrade your in-laws, friends, or their friends and relatives, or do you try to protect them? Are you honestly sweet and well-meaning, or are you either indifferent or plainly mean? Do you show negative streaks or do you actually try to be pleasant, sweet, encouraging, and helpful in the presence of your partner and otherwise? Do you talk behind your partner's or other people's backs?

4. *Common Interests and How to Handle Them.*

Do you try to establish common interests and then continue such interests, and handle them to the best advantage of all concerned, or are you just interested in what you alone are interested in, and try to force your partner to accept your, and neglect his, or her, interests? Is the form of entertainment which you select as entertaining and helpful to your loved one as it is to you? Do you attend and indulge in activities which may be more interesting to your partner than to yourself? Do you "feed" both of you mentally, as well as physically, and to the interests and likings and betterment of both concerned? Are the trips you take detrimental to one of you, or objected to by the relatives or friends of one? Do you cater excessively to your family and not to others? Do you have personal or family narcissism? Do you consult with each other with regard to entertainment, education, finances, health, advancement and family matters? In case of disagreement are you autocratic, or do you call in an arbitrator? In case of misunderstanding do you take genuine interest and time to explain your side of the situation? Do you permit yourself to be held down, to your detriment, without explaining the situation and doing something about it, or do you deliberately keep the other person back? Will your spouse give no reason under normal conditions? Does your spouse want to reason or is there too much outside influence?

5. *Vacations, Outings and Entertainment.*

Do you consider vacations, entertainment and outings important and do you consult each other about them? Or do you make up your mind about it yourself and insist that the other person must follow suit? Do you see both sides of the question, and particularly the other side? Are you difficult in regard to relinquishing your view-points or are you too prone to acquiesce?

Is it advisable to spend your vacations together or apart? Generally it is better that you be together, at least part of the vacation. If one of you can not go on vacation because of business, health, finances, or other reasons, shall the other one take the vacation anyhow? If you should separate because of vacations, how long should these separations last? Is it wise to have a long separation? All these questions have to be answered individually depending on circumstances. Generally, too long separations are inadvisable. Occasional and rarer separations may prove very valuable in exceptional cases. You must give yourself a chance to miss the other party. It results in a better appreciation, provided that the separation is no more than a week or two in duration and no longer, except under exceptional circumstances. Don't permit yourself to become too independent unless there is sickness, or frequent quarrels.

6. *Bedrooms.*

What about separate bedrooms? There are advantages and disadvantages, but there are more advantages on the side of separate bedrooms for a child or others in the family. By that is meant, the partners' bedroom should be separate from those of the other members of the family. It is very inadvisable for children to sleep in the same room with parents. It is considered bad mental hygiene. A man and wife should not have separate bedrooms except in case of certain illnesses.

Should there be separate beds? By all means it is advisable to have twin beds rather than one large bed. This will prove helpful physically, mentally and emotionally, and will maintain a better self-respect and independence on the part of both.

The location of the bedroom in relation to other bedrooms and other rooms in the house is important. It is preferable for the parents' bedroom to be on the second floor or at a distance from the kitchen and reception room. If possible, separate the parents' bedroom from the children's bedrooms with another room or two intervening. This will prove ideal, unless the children's bedrooms are on one floor and the parents' bedroom is on another floor, which may be better. Children should not have easy access to the parents' bedroom. At the same time, the bedroom should be a light, airy room and should not be easily accessible to visitors and others. The parents' bedroom should be more or less set aside as a "holy of holies."

7. *Discussions on Religion, Politics, and Business Matters.*

Discussions of religion, politics, business and other emotional and provocative matters should be limited. It is not wise to try to dissuade or change your partner's ideas. Be independent on these matters. A state of broad-mindedness is wholesome. Don't get into arguments about opinions pertaining to these topics. Even though you may convince the other person, it will not be a reward for your efforts, because it is very difficult to change people regarding their emotions. Even though you may change some, the effort is too strenuous and they may yet revert back to their own ideas. Then, too, there may be hard feelings and quarrels. Respect the other person. If you have no strong convictions, then you can readily and easily accept the ideas and opinions of your partner. It is all right to do so if the deviations are not very marked. Yet at the same time don't be a "jelly fish" and "swallow hook, line and sinker" everything your partner may expound without first considering it. If you are convinced that his or her opinion is better than yours, then accept it readily.

8. How Far Should Agreements or Disagreements be Carried?

Comprehensively, it is better to agree, if possible, but certainly the man should not be a "jelly fish." This also applies to the woman but not to such a degree. If the man is over-domineering, the woman must be very careful with regard to disagreements. It may be very essential that she agree, or at least not disagree, and for some time let matters take their course in order to get along. Then gradually, through the use of psychology, tact and understanding, she may be able to slowly win him over, so that it may not be compulsory to agree with him in everything. Occasionally, one disagrees with another person just to be disagreeable, to tease or worry the other person or to show up the person and prove one's own superiority. If the disagreements are true and genuine, and if there are no emotional upsets or dishonest motives involved, then the disagreements should continue until they are solved by reasoning or by consulting other sources. It is a mistake to try to solve disagreements through argument for the sake of arguing or for opportunistic motives. There will be some disagreements between most couples. If they are honest, non-neurotic and sensible, such disagreements are of little consequence. Ideally, there should be no disagreements, but ideals seldom exist. Ideals aim at goals which we strive to attain.

9. Joint Ownership of Property and Belongings.

Joint ownership of mutual possessions is a frequent occurrence and, at times, a necessity. Relatives and friends may bequeath or give property and belongings to one person, but only with the understanding that the belongings should be owned by one person and not by the other. It is likely that the gift will be accepted at the time, but at a later date one may want to borrow from the other, or may want to use temporarily (or otherwise) the partner's belongings or property, either for convenience or for necessity. Here is where troubles may start. If both partners are honest, sincere and in love, there will be no troubles. Otherwise, difficulties may arise. Then it may prove unprofitable to have accepted the other's contributions or assistance. At times, however, such a situation may result advantageously and lead to greater interest. It all depends on the various details. There are many couples who own property and belongings, either jointly or separately, and live happily and experience successful lives.

10. *Should Wives Work?*

Where there are children it is preferable that the wife should not work, but if there are no children and there is good health, it is advisable that the wife keep herself busy studying, teaching, doing social work, carrying out gainful work, but with the husband's consent. It is very easy for a wife to do nothing and deteriorate while her husband advances. It is the road of least resistance to do nothing, especially if one is well established financially, is fairly attractive, and imagines that one's health is not of the best. It is certainly more healthful to be active. For one to do a few minor things in the home and imagine this to be sufficient activity is a great mistake. It is not sufficient to reason thus: "If my husband makes enough money, I should not work or keep myself occupied." Excessive leisure leads to mental, physical, moral and social illness. On the other hand, if the wife insists on going to work, contrary to the husband's wishes, it may lead to arguments, separation or divorce. The question: "Should wives work?" depends on various elements and is a special case for every individual. Generally speaking, it should be remembered that a wife, whether she be financially able or not, should keep herself busy with various useful activities, or in time she will regret her stagnation and may even produce hardships and heartaches for others.

11. *Duties, Occupations and Financial Interests of Each.*

The duties, occupations and financial interests of each vary according to the individual circumstances. However, there should be definite duties for which each must be responsible. It is not wise for either to accept the duties of the other. Usually, it is wise for the husband to carry out the duties of earning a livelihood and to act as the head of the family. The wife is responsible for the household activities and the physical interests of the children as well as those of the entire family. The wife should also be responsible for the social activities of the family, always, of course, subject to her husband's convenience or consent. Both should consult each other regarding outings, trips, purchases which involve large finances, etc. Generally, neither the husband nor the wife should make purchases over the objections of the other. Neither should be extravagant. Both should cater to the ends of reasonable thrift and to that which will be agreeable to the conventions, particularly those which will contribute to mental, physical and emotional health. There must be definite duties established, recognized and adhered to by both. These duties and obligations may be carried out by the designated person, but if personal love exists, there may be an overlapping in functions. One should not tell the other, "These are your responsibilities and therefore I am out of it." If one is as capable as the other in doing a certain task, even though it is the duty of the other to perform it, yet if it is requested and is expedient for him to perform the task, it should be done without objection or resentment. Each should be concerned with the interests, activities and duties of the other, but shouldn't interfere with the carrying out of such activities if resented by the other. This subject is largely a question of co-operation, understanding, duty, efficiency and love. A few violations of the above may not be serious.

12. *Vocations, Professions and Businesses*

Many women who are either in love or are married may not be trained professionally or vocationally and may not have had definite experience in business. It may not be necessary to have such training and experience. There are, however, a number of exceptions: The basis of such situations may be explained by stating that in the past it has been advisable for a woman to remain dependent upon a man, so that she could look up to the man and be more cooperative. Then, too, it may be difficult to have two captains on the same boat, or two cooks in the same kitchen, both with equal powers and duties. Therefore, man being better trained, woman had to yield, and in this way there was one strong efficient captain in each family. Also, it may have been intended for woman to concentrate on giving birth and rearing children. This has been woman's vocation and occupation as well as her business. Since man is not biologically capable of such activity, it has been forced upon woman. There is no doubt that woman can become as proficient as man when necessary. There are many women who are outstanding in various fields, but since nature has equipped woman better than man for her natural duty of motherhood, she naturally leans toward that function.

There are, however, some women who are incapable of bearing children, and adoption is contra-indicated. There are other couples who should remain childless because of physical, social or mental reasons. It may be advisable for a woman to be childless when the head of the family is lost, or is expected to be lost, either by death or accident, or other reasons, and where it is necessary for the woman to play the role of the man also, professionally or vocationally. It is therefore advisable, in these complicated and critical days, for women to know something of business and the professions. Nature has so endowed woman that in times of stress and necessity, if she is prepared, she may become as capable as man. Ordinarily, a woman shouldn't be too anxious to marry early. She should first work and become acquainted with the business or professional world. She may then be better able to advise her husband, as well as her children, and in the event circumstances force her to be both father and mother, she will be able to face the emergency. If she is not prepared, the entire family may be demoralized. A woman is the stabilizing factor in the home, if she is properly prepared. If she is not prepared, she may become the unstabilizing factor and blame her weaknesses upon her husband.

Time was when it was considered disgraceful for a woman to know about business matters. It was a disgrace for girls to work. Men seldom discussed business matters with their wives or other female members of the family. However, the world has changed. Women today compete with men. At times it is inadvisable to compete with men, but circumstances have forced women to do so. They are not only mothers, but are frequently the advisers and providers. Although women have been considered inferior to men because they were not prepared, it is now being recognized that women are equal to men, or superior in some respects, if they are prepared. In grammar and in high schools, the fair sex excels. Many women excel in college, and properly prepared women who have been trained efficiently have excelled in large business organizations, in politics and on the stage.

If they take advantage of the opportunities to prepare themselves and if they are encouraged, women have the mentality and ability to carry on as well as men. For various reasons, there are some women who prefer to compete with men, and there are also many who shun and fear such competition. Because of the present world situation, women should not be discouraged or excluded from the professions, vocations and various occupations of men. Ordinarily, this will not make men jealous and it will not interfere with love affairs. Should a woman find that her husband is well able to provide for her, she can gradually retire to her normal role, namely, motherhood and the rearing of children, as well as general advisor and source of inspiration to her entire family.

Where circumstances appear assured, it is better for a woman to prepare herself physically through athletics, music, dancing, gymnastics, etc., as well as in the arts which deal with special music, elocution, the appreciation of aesthetics, and become an expert in the understanding of personality traits and character. A woman's intuition, if honest, is often better than man's reason.

13. *Should Friends and Relatives Be Taken into the Home and Under What Circumstances?*

This is often an individual case and the answer depends on the special conditions. If there is a choice, it is better to live away from relatives rather than in the same home. It may be helpful to live in the neighborhood or in the same building with some friends and relatives, but very seldom in the same house or same apartment. If it is a private home and not in the same apartment, this may be permissible too, if there are no interference, conflicts, criticisms and domineering. Certainly, one should not live with his in-laws or with his own relatives, unless he is still single. If there is an unfortunate situation, such as the death of one of the parents, thus leaving one parent, and there is ample space in which the surviving person may live, it may be advisable to take this person into one's home, providing this individual has not been a troublemaker, and providing the probabilities are that he will not cause conflicts with the family. The same applies to brothers, sisters, aunts and even close friends. One shouldn't be too selfish. It may even be essential to take into one's home one or more refugees from the war-stricken countries. This all depends on the finances, conveniences, health and circumstances which surround these situations.

If there is a choice of placing the relatives or friends in another home, which is convenient and has a nice environment, then it is better to pay such rental as is necessary and affordable and permit one's own home to remain uncrowded and free from encroachment. One shouldn't be too prone to accept relatives and friends as permanent residents, unless the person accepted is fine, tactful and will prove cooperative, and if he is alone and needs the companionship of his benefactor. It is also essential that the home be sufficiently spacious to accommodate such an addition and that the husband and wife are mutually willing to accept such an addition. It must not be forgotten that many a quarrel and even a broken home has resulted from situations in which a relative or friend was taken into the home as a permanent resident. Should you accept such a person to live with you, be sure that he has a definite understanding as to what part of the house he is assigned to, his duties, obligations, privileges, and the definite role which he is to play in the home. This understanding from the outset must be clear and definitely agreed upon by all concerned.

14. *What Are Some Things to Say or Do, to Keep Each Other in Good Humor?*

Don't discuss things which the other person dislikes, or which might cause either ill feelings, resentfulness or unpleasantness. Discuss things which the other person is interested in and likes, or that which will boost his ego and produce pleasantness and harmony. Don't give the other person digs. Don't disagree, torment or embarrass the other person. Be kind, encouraging, decent, harmonious, helpful and honest, in general. Conduct yourself in a manner that will make your partner feel secure, desired, important and happy. Do both little and big things for the other person which will prove to be the interest of both, with consideration and love. In case of arguments, take your partner's side unless you see gross error and injustice. Try to end the argument quickly; but later, in a tactful manner, reason out the situation and courteously show your partner his error. Do not treat your loved one, as if everything is taken for granted. Courtesies and considerations must be shown continually. Remain a lover at all ages. *Do not talk or associate with your partner's enemies, or those who are not liked by your loved one, unless this dislike is unreasonable and unmerited.* Then try to adjust it, if you can, without too many complications.

Spend some time alone with your partner, but be sure that you don't overdo it. Say and do the things which will make you two somewhat dependent upon each other, but not excessively so. *Call each other endearing names, and do not be sarcastic even though it may be in jest. Do not belittle your partner's relatives or friends.* If you have something good to say about them, do so. Show your partner's good points, fine qualities, accomplishments and ambitions. *Avoid revealing his inequalities, past mistakes and unfortunate incidents.* Be sentimental, remember birthdays, anniversaries and pleasant reminders. Remember your partner with gifts, favors and kind, encouraging remarks.

15. *At Social Events, if One Wants to Go Home, Should the Other Go Also?*

At social events, if the two arrive together, they should certainly leave together. If one behaves abnormally, which makes it advisable for one to leave, both should leave together, regardless of which one is responsible. If the misbehavior is caused by one, and is repeated, then it may be advisable for only one to attend future social events, or one may leave and the other may remain. However, this is applicable only when the ill-behavior has been repeated at least a number of times. Frequently one misbehaves and should be held responsible for this misbehavior. However, the other partner may very often be equally or even more responsible. Under such circumstances, both should leave together, or avoid such circumstances at social affairs. If one wants to go home for any reason, even though this reason may not be known to the other, both should leave together. Then the matter should be thrashed out unemotionally and honestly as to the reason why the departure took place.

16. *Should A Woman Permit Herself to Outdo Her Husband Socially, Professionally or Financially?*

If her husband shows no serious objections, it may be permissible. Generally, however, it is not advisable because according to our present civilization, the husband usually takes the lead and shouldn't "take a back seat" to his wife, except under very unusual circumstances.

When the wife takes the lead, quarrels, arguments and unhappiness frequently follow. This applies more to social and professional leadership than it does to finances. Yet it may also apply to investments and various stock transactions. There may be jealousies between husband and wife or sweethearts, if they are in the same profession, or depend on the same art for a livelihood or recognition. Custom is an institution resulting from experience and therefore it is advisable to follow it, even though occasionally there is room for exceptions. Thus, if there is a possibility of competition in any manner, it is better for the wife to permit her husband to take the lead.

17. *Incapacitation of Partner.*

(a) If your partner becomes hopelessly incapacitated, is it your duty to stick by him or her? The answer is yes. If your previous relationship has been honest and worthwhile, you should stick by your partner.

(b) Should the incapacitated partner encourage you to stick by him, or should you be given your freedom? The incapacited partner should not encourage you to stick by him. However, even though you may be urged to take your freedom, you should reject it and stick to your loved one, providing, as stated above, your previous relations have been pleasant and worthwhile.

There are a few exceptions: if you discover that you have been deceived, your obligations can be questionable. If your partner is suffering from a chronic disease, which may infect or incapacitate you and authoritative sources have so advised, and if you have done all in your power to help your unfortunate partner, and if you can do no more, you should make yourself free. If your partner dies, you must live on and happily as best you can.

If your loved one receives a life jail sentence and, after strenuous efforts, you have been unsuccessful in freeing him and have been informed through authoritative sources that a life incarceration is certain, you should set yourself free.

If your loved one has become afflicted mentally, so that authorities assure you that the case is absolutely hopeless, and if you are convinced that it is impossible for him to live a normal existence again, you should set yourself free.

XIII

Why Men Become Promiscuous

It is claimed, more or less universally, that man by nature is polygamous and therefore may be more inclined toward promiscuity than woman.

If a man is negative about his mother, although he may sincerely believe he is in love with his wife, he may have unconscious yearnings to be promiscuous, so as to castigate both his wife and mother.

If he is negative about his father, he may be promiscuous because unconsciously he likes to disgrace his father.

Sometimes a man's promiscuity can be blamed on his wife's physical weakness, her denials and her inability to satisfy him physically, mentally, and particularly, emotionally.

By nature, man may be more curious than woman, or at least he may be more inclined to give vent to his curiosity through promiscuity. It is easier for a man to be promiscuous than for a woman because he has less at stake, and for some unknown reasons the taboo on man is certainly not as great as it is on woman. Right or wrong, we must admit the truth—that the double standard does prevail.

An unattached man, who for some reason is surrounded by an environment of a number of women who admire him for physical, mental, financial or other reasons, may become promiscuous if he lacks the will-power or emotional stability to withstand temptation.

Unconscious homosexual feelings in a man, doubts as to his masculinity, feelings of sexual and personal inferiorities, or a "sissy defense mechanism" may encourage a man's pseudo-defense by his indulging either in bragging about his physical abilities or in actual promiscuity.

Conscious or unconscious hatred against women, *rather than excessive love*, may be an underlying cause of a man's promiscuity.

A wife who nags and belittles her husband and uses negative suggestion, or who pays too much attention to her children and others, or who fails to praise and encourage the husband, may force him to seek sexual outlets elsewhere. Or, he may at least start out to seek only admiration, affection, praise, encouragement, security, relaxation, and wind up by becoming promiscuous.

In conclusion, *a wife who is physically normal, who understands her own psychology and that of her husband, who caters to him in every way, who is completely honest with him, who uses positive suggestion and thus endeavors to make an "angel" of him, who knows how to get along with people and who understands the sexual technique, is able to keep her husband faithful to her—if she is married to a normal man.*

XIV

Why Women Become Promiscuous

Women become promiscuous when they are sexually frigid.

Sometimes they do so when they are dissatisfied with their partners, either physically, economically, mentally or emotionally.

Another reason revolves around an adult woman being negative about her father, so that when she identifies a man with her father, she may become promiscuous in order to "punish" her father. Or, she may become promiscuous in order to "punish" her husband, consciously or unconsciously. She may give other reasons for her conduct, but these reasons involve rationalizations.

A husband who frequently makes his wife jealous or who is promiscuous, and is so discovered by his wife, and if he neglects her sexually, mentally, physically and socially, then he encourages her to become promiscuous. If her husband mistreats her in any form or manner, neglects her, is cruel to her, blames her excessively for many things, or does not know how to handle her psychologically, thus making her chronically unhappy, the woman may become promiscuous.

A husband who talks too much about sex may arouse in his wife too much curiosity. This curiosity, coupled with other indiscretions, such as belittling her, degrading her, not considering her likes and dislikes, failing to make sacrifices for her, etc., may result in promiscuity on the part of the woman.

College girls who are brought up loosely or who were

strongly over- or under-protected or who were made to feel excessively inferior or excessively curious and then are sent out-of-town for their college studies often succumb to the male college students and "shack up" during week ends and at other times and indulge in sex frequently. In this manner, their curiosities are satisfied, they get even with their parents, and feel that they are grown up. This is more common now because of the sophistication regarding contraception through pills and other means. Girls' curiosity is easily satisfied especially if they are distant from their homes. A number get pregnant in spite of this knowledge and the parents never know it. Some parents buy birth control pills for their daughters; some fathers even get doctors to help procure women for their sons and either instruct or ask a doctor to instruct their sons in methods of contraception and V.D. prevention.

XV

Bad Habits

Although it is possible for one person to reform his or her partner through companionship and marriage, the usual role is that if reformation does take place, it is of a temporary nature only. A man or woman who has been a chronic alcoholic may stop drinking temporarily, but when difficulties, troubles or problems present themselves, the necessity for escape will prevail and drinking will be resumed.

The same psychology applies to the use of narcotics, but to a greater degree. A chronic alcoholic or drug addict may have a brilliant personality, but the escape patterns are so strong that sooner or later he must resort to alcohol, drugs, or both.

As a rule, such people are psychopathic personalities, and are not insane or feeble-minded. Since it is not possible to guarantee anyone an easy future, and since the possibilities are that emotional strain may be expected, one can be more inclined to believe that relapses will follow.

It is not wise to rationalize that "if I love him, or if he loves me sufficiently, alcohol and drug addiction will never be resorted to again." Experience teaches that relapses are more often the rule than the exception.

It is less likely for a thief to continue stealing after a love marriage or during a love state. However, if one has resorted to continued thievery and gambling, the possibilities are that this may continue whether he is discovered or not. Such behavior is ingrained in the character and is an unfortunate and discouraging condition. Again, it can be said that a love affair or marriage may cause a temporary cessation, but sooner or later dishonesty will be resumed. If the individual is one of high intelligence, such behavior may remain unnoticed or undetected by those who love him for a long period. If the intelligence is not so high, the person will be unable to disguise his behavior, which will result in an earlier detection.

The causes of addiction, thievery and gambling are both conscious and unconscious, and are deeply rooted. By a prolonged and deeply technical psychotherapy, it may be possible to correct such anti-social behavior in some cases. It usually cannot be done through religion or the pleadings of the loved one, but it may be accomplished through the proper psychotherapy or psychoanalysis with the complete cooperation of the family. Although one may find a rare exception, one should never depend on the eventuality of a complete cure of a psychopath.

On the subject of promiscuity, this failing often disappears during a love affair and a love marriage, providing the promiscuity is not based on such causes as sexual perversion or other sexual deviations, or based on definite hatreds toward the father or mother, or toward society, and if the person is not an advanced psychopath.

If there are definite sexual abnormalities, be they organic or psychological, and if there are definite hatreds (conscious or unconscious), the probability is that promiscuity will be continued, because sooner or later a loophole will be found which will be combined with some sort of rationalization, and the excuse will finally lead the person to do that which he has done in the past. Patterns of behavior are repetitive in various kinds of people.

Other bad habits and practices will likely be continued unless the individuals are truly in love and are capable of maintaining such a state. If the love or infatuation is of a sudden and temporary nature, which seems to be the case many times, then the individual will relapse to his former bad habits. If the person has a fine character and a low neurotic index, and if his or her partner behaves similarly, in addition to being very cooperative and encouraging, and if there are no strained outside factors—the possibilities are that the bad habits will disappear or improve. In time, the couple will get used to each other, improve each other, become dependent upon each other, develop common interests, learn from each other, and improve their general characters and behavior.

If each one actively maintains the likes and dislikes of the other through study, understanding, common interests, love, appreciation and a knowledge of the psychology of the other, and if there is catering to each other emotionally, mentally and physically—the likelihood is that neither one will look for escape of various kinds or for the company of others. If, on the other hand, one is neglectful of the other and makes little or no attempt at understanding or co-operating with the other, whether it be conscious or unconscious—then one or both will eventually look for escape and for the company and admiration of others. Once you have gained love, study and practice how to hold it!

XVI
Jealousy

Jealousy is a very important cause of rifts between lovers and divorces among married people. Jealousy may be precipitated in one member by the other one deliberately, by failing to prevent it, or by sheer neglect or indifference. It is normal for all children and adults to be jealous, but the degrees vary and so do the stimulating causes.

Jealousy is an emotion which has been developed in a person both consciously and unconsciously. The child who experiences jealous rages a number of times throughout life by witnessing parents and other relatives or friends going through such emotions will be more inclined to be jealous also. This is especially true if the person entertains strong elements of *inferiority, insecurity* and possibly conscious or unconscious *guilt feelings*. In other words—he suffers from the unholy trinity.

If an individual feels secure and has confidence in himself, the problem of jealousy will be remote. For example: if I believe that I am as good looking, as healthy, as smart, as well-educated, as important and as efficient as my rival, or if I think I excel my rival, there will be only the slightest possibility of my becoming jealous. However, should I think that others excel me in looks, in education, health, station in life, capabilities and other valuable assets, and if I am very much interested in my rivals, then there will be no doubt as to my jealousy.

Any doubts as to one's qualities or defects are not only conscious but unconscious as well. Inferiorities, insecurities, and guilt feelings are usually both conscious and unconscious.

When a couple exhibits great deviations or marked differences socially, chronologically, educationally or otherwise, there will be sufficient loopholes and opportunities for *jealousy*. Frequently, jealousy and jealous rages are not recognized as such, but are misinterpreted as other situations.

One of the commonest causes of maladjustment and incompatibility is the existence and exemplification of various degrees of jealousy and their influences on behavior. Mild degrees of jealousy are normal and frequently are of no serious consequences. It is the extreme degree of jealousy which breaks up a couple or produces serious damage.

XVII

The Technique of Withdrawing from a Love Affair

1. First be sure that you have good, honest reasons for withdrawing from the affair.
2. Convince yourself that it will not hurt you or the other party, but it may prove mutually advantageous under your circumstances.
3. Don't evade the situation by vanishing from the scene or prolonging it excessively. Instead, face it, explain the situation to your partner and bring it to a conclusion.
4. However, don't act impulsively. Act only after you have given the matter your careful consideration.
5. Although you should listen to the advice of others, be sure that you make up your own mind rather than depend completely on the advice of friends.
6. Frequently it is wise to discuss such problems with those who have had more experience than you have had.
7. Be sure that you consider all the reasons for and against breaking with your partner and don't be one-sided.
8. Don't be guided by your emotions only, but incorporate reason and logic in your decision.
9. Once you have decided to break, do so firmly, promptly, and with no regrets.
10. After you have parted, don't disparage or even discuss your partner with your friends or relatives, and don't give any reasons or excuses for the break, other than you both decided it was the best procedure.

XVIII

Sex in the Unmarried and Married

Whether it is remembered or not, the majority of people after pubescence have sexual experiences which are either provoked or unprovoked. By "provoked" is meant onanism (self-abuse) or masturbation. These are normal situations and there should be no guilt feelings attached to such acts. It is *untrue* that such actions result in insanity, paresis, paralysis, and other diseases. If this were true, practically everybody would be insane or paralyzed. The chief or only damage of masturbation is in misinformation and the guilt feelings which may result. The guilt feelings may cause serious troubles when one is young and when one is old. If there are no guilt feelings, there is absolutely no damage or injury resulting from such actions. If one indulges too often, there may be some feelings of fatigue or sleepiness, but even these symptoms may not follow. On the other hand, it is not absolutely necessary to indulge in masturbation. One can be perfectly normal and happy without masturbation. After marriage, it is inadvisable to continue such practices. There are many adults and married people who indulge in masturbation and in heterosexual and homosexual activities. This is not advisable. It is preferable to indulge in heterosexual activities only.

By "unprovoked" sex activity is meant a sexual orgasm which occurs involuntarily while one is asleep. This phenomenon is very often normal and found to exist in people who do not indulge themselves sexually. No damage results from such experiences and there should be no alarm about it. Why not consider it on this basis? A container is filled with sexual fluid and gradually, as it is overfilled, it overflows. There can be no damage from such experiences.

XIX

Sex During Courtship

According to convention, persons are not supposed to enjoy sex with each other during courtship or with others. But, if the truth is to be known, although it may once have been very rare and uncommon for couples to engage sexually during courtship in the past, it is very common now and has been for many years. Although most married couples would not admit it, a large number of them enjoyed sex during their courtship. Although it is better to refrain from such practices, many couples are just as happy and are as much in love in spite of the fact that they have indulged during courtship. A number of couples have confessed to me that they are convinced that they would not have been married except for premarital relationships. Other couples admitted that a premarital relation might have prevented their marriages. Then there are couples with marital infelicities who have had premarital relationships. It is not believed that premarital relationships increase or decrease love possibilities, but it is known that relationships before and during courtship are increasing rapidly in number. Some people object to long engagements because of this. Yet the evils of brief engagements before marriage may be greater than the evils of lengthy engagements. Again, here it is easy to over-estimate sex. If the couples are well prepared and are finely developed for love and marriage, then love and marriage will follow, whether there have been premarital relationships or not.

The question may be asked, should a man or woman indulge sexually with others prior to marriage and during courtship? The religious and conventional answer would be, no. The practical answer, which takes cognizance of existing conditions, would be, yes, for most men, and, yes, for many women. If it is possible to carry out such practices without the consequences of venereal disease, pregnancy, and social ostracism, and if the information is not discussed and does not reach the marital partners' relatives and friends, there may be no consequences, especially if the marital partners are not puritanical.

In previous generations, one could advise a courting couple to ask their parents, relatives and friends for advice with regard to sex before marriage. In these days, it is better advice to tell such a couple to consult reliable physicians and authoritative books.

XX

Sex in Marriage

All couples contemplating marriage should be examined physically and mentally by reliable physicians, and should have blood tests. Examining physicians should answer various questions for the couples and perhaps write out certain information, or refer them to certain books, dispel any existing fears, superstitions, misinformation or erroneous ideas, and advise the couple of the consequences. Most people who get married these days are well acquainted with sex, but need some special guidance and advice. The first sexual acts should be performed with tenderness, and the couple should have their minds made up as to whether they are to use contraception or not. The act must be carried out the first few times in such a manner that there should be no pain or roughness, no remembrances of unpleasantness left; for if the first few acts are painful, one of the two people may remain partially frigid. There should be plenty of lubrication, patience, a knowledge of what is happening, trust, confidence and love.

The frequency of sexual intercourse should depend more or less on the health of both parties and the urge, as well as upon the advice of the physician. The average frequency is two or three times per week at the beginning of marriage, then the frequency is reduced. It is better underdone than overdone. An average normal adult may be able to indulge once in twenty-four hours every day in the week, but with some people, this may cause loss in weight, a tired feeling, excessive sleepiness and a much lowered physical resistance, which may in turn cause serious illness. Others may be unable to indulge more than one or twice a week and therefore the frequency may have to be reduced. Where there is a tendency toward impotence, illness or weakness in the male, the frequency must be reduced. In many women there is some degree of frigidity during early marriage which may gradually disappear; while in others, the frigidity may come on after some years of marriage. Some couples develop psychological impotence and frigidity because of fear of pregnancy. With the use of the pessary, pills and other reliable contraceptive measures, there need be no fear of pregnancy. If pregnancy takes place, relations may continue even to the sixth or seventh month, but generally it ceases after the fifth month. There are always exceptions. Some people may cease relationships after a few months of pregnancy, and others may continue even through the eighth month.

Many cases of impotence and frigidity have no physical relationship, since they are entirely psychological. Although there are some physical causes of impotence and frigidity, it is more common for the young and middle-aged to suffer psychic impotence and psychic frigidity, which are unconscious in origin. If one understands positive and negative Oedipus and Electra complexes and positive and negative fixations, homosexuality or bisexuality and perversions, it will be easier to understand psychic impotence and psychic frigidity. For further writings on the subject, consult books on psychoanalysis, unconscious psychology and homosexuality.

It is wise for women, and particularly married women, to douche weekly or daily. The douche can consist of hot water, or fifteen to twenty drops of Lysol in several quarts of water. Daily douches should be encouraged for cleansing purposes, just as tooth brushing or mouth rinsing is important for good hygiene. Some gynecologists are against this but I have known numerous women who have followed my advice for over thirty years and they are married, healthy, clean and free from irritating discharges.

It is preferable not to have intercourse during menstruation. However, there are a number of people who do during menstruation, with no ill effects and with no impregnations during these periods. Contrary to the beliefs of many people that douching is harmful during menstruation, the fact is that douching at such times is beneficial, unless strong medications are used. If one is inclined to menstruate excessively, then perhaps douching should be omitted. Ordinarily, a hot douche is very good every day of the month, regardless of menstruation, and even during it.

There need be no fear of the normal menopause or that which follows pelvic operations, or normal menopause at the ages of thirty-nine through forty-nine, when women gradually cease menstruating. This is a normal process, and although there may be some symptoms, such as hot flushes, nervousness and variations during the menstrual period, nothing of major seriousness happens. The menopause period can be minimized as to its effects by injections of certain glandular preparations or certain pills by mouth, but even these may not be necessary. Just before, during, and shortly after the menopause, many women become strongly sexed. Some develop mental symptoms around this period, largely because of fears, superstitions, anxieties, feelings of guilt and misinformation. Those women who become demented at this period have been abnormal before their menopause. There is no reason why the menopause should make a gigantic change in a woman's life, any more than the onset of menstruation in a girl of thirteen or fourteen years of age should cause her to be psychotic, except that a few days before and during the menses women may be irritable, tense and show emotional strain. Sometimes the words "premenstrual tension" may be used. If the attitudes have been and are normal, the mental and emotional conditions during menstrual and the climacteric states should not deviate to serious degrees.

With reference to extra-marital relations on the part of the male and the female—conventions, society and the church, condemn it. Extra-marital relations do interfere with the love life of a couple, even though we know that in this modern day there are frequent occurrences, mostly on the part of the male. They lessen the emotional ties, confidence and love feelings. In some cases, they may create hatred and destroy love. In other cases, the effect may be little but cause similar behavior in the spouse. In still other cases, there may be a temporary reduction in the degree of love between the couple; later love may be converted into hatred, or it may return and become intensified. There are some couples who agree for a short period to permit one or both to indulge in extra-marital relationships, but usually these agreements are shortlived, and are generally not advisable. Although promiscuous sexual relationships are frequent occurrences with unmarried people, promiscuity also exists with married people, but with much less frequency. The reasons for promiscuity have already been described in this volume. There are a number of ideal couples who have never been promiscuous. This number has decreased, as compared to the larger numbers of past generations. Promiscuity is more influenced by psychology, physiology, and sociology than it is by religion, but religion has strong influences in keeping couples from indulging in promiscuity. If we rear children with good physical and mental hygienic backgrounds and teach normal love among ourselves and our neighbors, there will be more love, a better love, less promiscuity, and a saner religion will be practiced, with the end result that there will be more happiness.

XXI
Divorce

When a couple disagrees, neither one should consult a lawyer for a long period. It is frequent that although the lawyer may mean well, more complications are likely to result. Sometimes it may be advisable for both to discuss the situation with relatives first, before seeing a lawyer. However relatives are usually too prone to side with their own, for blood is thicker than water. Too many relatives become prejudiced too easily. At times, consulting an experienced and understanding physician may help; and, less frequently, consulting a clergyman may be of useful service. The best possible method however, if practical, is for the two not only to consult a psychoanalyst, but to actually be psychoanalyzed. This does not mean going to a psychiatrist or a psychologist, or even an analyst. It does mean consulting a psychoanalyst who will have to be seen for approximately one to three years, making three or more visits per week. While studying oneself under the guidance of the psychoanalyst, there can be no definite decisions made regarding the marital status. After one year or longer, the couple will know what to do and they will know better than anyone else. They will not need the advice of relatives, friends, lawyers, or anybody else. It must be repeated here that lawyers and courts frequently make such situations worse. This is true to the extent that the entanglement may make the problem almost insoluble. LAWYERS AND COURTS USUALLY SEE THE LEGAL SIDE, WHICH IS USUALLY NOT THE QUESTION AT ALL. A physician may only see the physical side, which is also not the question. The relatives will see the emotional and financial side, which are usually not the most important elements either.

Many, or all of these situations, may be due in a small part to external reasons, but the real trouble is a psychological one, which needs thorough understanding and re-education. It is not only a matter of conscious psychology, personal development, with character involvements, ignorance and misinformation, but it is largely an understanding of one's own unconscious. This may be difficult for some people to see or understand. Those who have studied unconscious psychology and have applied it to themselves can readily see the point, and can evaluate the tremendous importance of this situation. One does not have to have a marital infelicity, be neurotic or maladjusted, in order to require analysis. Normal, fine people, can also reap great benefits from an analysis. Yet those who deviate psychologically, emotionally, mentally and socially, and who are surrounded by serious problems must be analyzed in order to solve their problems adequately. It must be reiterated that the best means of solving one's problems, if practical, is to undergo a thorough psychoanalysis, and if there is an analyst in the city where the person resides, well and good. If not, many persons should borrow money and move temporarily to a city where there is a competent psychoanalyst. If one member of the family is psychoanalyzed, it is certainly very advantageous for the others to do so also. After both are analyzed, even though there may have been disagreements, the serious probability is that marital infelicity and love difficulties will disappear, even though it may be necessary to face strenuous circumstances. These statements may appear biased, but having seen and experienced repeatedly such situations, these conclusions are the normal and logical summation. Even though it may be conceded that there are other methods which may prove successful, these are real possibilities but not always probabilities. Those who have not been psychoanalyzed themselves and have not had concrete practical experiences with this type of work, may not understand these conclusions, or may even disagree. On the other hand, those who have been psycho-analyzed and have had these experiences directly themselves, will have to concur with these conclusions.

Finally, the reasons which individuals give to themselves and others are usually not the real reasons for divorce, and if complaints do exist, they may be ignored, minimized and eliminated, if there is the proper psychological understanding, with outside interferences by family and associates.

When it is found necessary to go through with a divorce, because of good mental, physical, and social reasons; and it is certain that these conclusions were not drawn hastily; and it appears impossible to live a happy existence; and all this is the final result of much clear thinking, guidance and patience, then there should be no guilt feelings or hesitation about a divorce, regardless of what anybody will think. Many who divorce have guilt feelings before, during, and after the divorce. This is unfortunate and in time may cause many hardships for all concerned. The attitude toward divorce should be the same as toward the separation of two partners who find it impossible to continue in business. Or, it should be the same as a person who finally decides (after considerable deliberation) that his business is a losing proposition and must gradually continue from bad to worse. The decision is then made that an end must be sought, and the sooner the better. There should be no guilt or peculiar feelings about it. If it is the right thing, then it should be done immediately and be gotten over with.

There are some people who make mistakes by marrying the wrong people. The continuation of such mistakes is senseless, especially if one's religion permits divorce. The fact that a mistake was made during youth or otherwise, doesn't mean that the two people and their children must suffer for their remaining days. Many people who have divorced have remarried and lived happily afterwards. This does not mean that if two people have difficulties in getting along, or if they disagree, they should become divorced, and if they remarry they will live happily afterwards. There are some people who divorce and remarry several times, but are never happy. They should not be married at all. They are neurotic or have psychopathic traits which are unrecognized by the person or persons involved, and they usually blame their partners for their difficulties and cannot see where the primary causes of these difficulties lie.

It is not necessary that a married person remain married to his partner for life, when there is unhappiness, quarrels, disagreements, and hard feelings. Likewise, it is not necessary to divorce and get remarried, if the person has traits which may keep this individual from being happy with others under average conditions. Frequently, a person who divorces one will have troubles with another, and divorce again, and remain miserable. A very keen psychiatrist, or better, a psychoanalyst, may be able to straighten out such an individual, so that the divorce may be prevented and the person may improve to such a degree that divorce may be unnecessary or another marriage may be a happy one. Otherwise, such a person should remain single and not have any guilt feelings about it. His attitude should be that "I am the type of person who should remain single and I shall do the right thing about it, be a sport, do the best I can, and live alone and like it."

There are all types of people on this earth. Some should get married and have children. Some should get married and have no children, and some should stay single.

XXII

Hints on Getting Along

For man and woman to get along properly, it is essential to understand how to solve their individual and common problems, just the same as it is important for students, business men, and professional individuals, who are to be successful. If there is an inability to understand and solve problems, sooner or later the couple will be in serious trouble and the proper feelings toward each other and love, may be seriously impaired or be made impossible. Therefore, these suggestions, if properly understood, may prove helpful.

1. First, recognize the existence of the problem and try to understand it thoroughly, so that you can define it in your own words, and understand its limitations, scope and consequences. State the problem clearly in your own words and try to explain it to yourself, and your partner, so that both of you can see clearly just what the issue is, or what the situation is with its barriers, limits and meanings? This must be very clear, and there should be no wishful thinking or rationalizations about its limits, scope or importance.

2. Compare your definition of the problem with that of your partner and see whether you agree or disagree and in what respects.

3. Write down the various elements concerning your problem and enumerate them, as well as list the facts which may have any bearing or associations with the problem and try to give each element its relative weight and importance. Compare your evaluations with your partner's.

4. You may suddenly or gradually see one or more ways of solving the problem. Compare your method of solution with your partner's, but don't close your mind to your methods or his. Don't assume an argumentative attitude or become too passive. Don't assume or take for granted that either you or your partner must domineer the situation. After you have considered the various methods of solution, wait a while and at some future time (according to circumstances) let the methods roll over in your mind and finally come to a conclusion.

5. Before actually putting into practice your solution, study the consequences and the results of the different methods. Compare the different approaches and different results through imagination. Try to keep in mind that the method used should be practical and should not involve exhibitionism or inefficiency. Although it may not be necessary to come to a quick solution, don't postpone your problem indefinitely, for time may draw interest and aggravate the problem. Sometimes, time alone solves or makes the problem easier, but don't be too eager to depend on this element of postponement.

6. It is better not to use the "trial and error" method for solving your problems. Study, think out your problem and take advice from authoritative sources, and finally do personal reasoning. Many mistakes are made by using the "trial and error" method. Once you have decided the method to be used for solving the problem or problems, don't hesitate. Exert your efforts, resources and abilities for an immediate solution.

7. Once the problem has been solved, remember the methods used so that you can profit in the future by the experience. If unsuccessful, don't give up the task but try to discover why the problem wasn't solved properly. See where there were errors in judgment and where there was misinformation. Try to discover why the method used did not function and set about to change the methods so that your problem can be solved successfully, rather than depend on luck, fate, or leave the problem discouragingly unsolved.

Don't shun problems. Assume the attitude that all normal and successful people have problems. Don't run away from them but become keener and better because you have solved problems. Know how to tackle others in the future. The ability to face problems and solve them properly is a splendid trait and is most desirable.

In order to help assure a better, more permanent, and happier love, try to prevent, or endeavor to get rid of destructive habits and attitudes. A person is better liked by all if there is a general habit of honesty, and there is developed an attitude of truthfulness in this person. Don't permit the various habits or patterns of escaping reality through excessive drinking, unnecessary medicine, sleeping, sickness, gambling, gossip, excessive reading, or by spending too much time with games or hobbies. Don't permit the attitude that a man's place is in his office or at work, while a woman's place is in the kitchen, or that a man must be responsible for the finances and education of the family, while the woman has no part of this, but instead the woman's responsibility is bearing children and catering to them, and this ends her duties and responsibilities. Remember that duties often should, and do, over-lap, according to circumstances. Don't permit yourself to assume a pessimistic and grouchy attitude, or be periodically moody or emotionally unstable. Try to remain pleasant and keep your emotions under control regardless of business reverses and troubles in the home. In other words, be reliable and stable.

Assume the attitude and belief of never criticizing your relatives, friends and associates, except under the most unusual circumstances. If something derogatory is to be said about relatives and others, many times you will find yourself the winner if nothing is said. Just leave it unsaid. Establish the attitude that it does not pay to be an exhibitionist. Don't spend extra money, or buy articles not needed, or say and do things for impressions only. In the long run "exhibitionism" and special activities for impressions don't pay. When things don't go your way or if you make mistakes don't look for a "goat"; don't blame others. If you left a loophole and even though others are responsible, you are also responsible. Don't give excuses. Admit the truth. Understand it and try in the future not to repeat it. Remember we all make mistakes, and we should be big enough to admit them. It is very easy to find excuses and blame someone, for our failures and mistakes.

When appointments are made try to keep them. If you are late or forget the appointment, don't belittle it, neglect the situation, or lie about it—tell the truth.

Don't praise your friend's enemies in his presence. Neither should you belittle his friends. If you want to correct your friend or your partner because you find it necessary to do so, you must be most tactful. Be sure you are not doing it to "show him up," in order to elevate yourself, or to dig at your friend by belittling others.

Don't tell your partner how wonderful your ex-boyfriends or ex-girlfriends were, or are. Sometimes it may not be damaging to boast of successes, but there you are treading on dangerous territory because jealousy may show itself. Prevent jealousy. Don't lift yourself up by hurting your partner or others. In general, if you have no serious complexes, no inferiorities, no prejudices, no jealousies, no "axe to grind," no guilt feelings, and no insecurities, and if you are honest and really love your partner, you will neither favor nor do anything in your own defense, or for purposes of lifting yourself up, which will hurt your partner's feelings, prejudices, and his pleasure principle.

Now that you have some valuable ideas in getting along with your partner with reference to correct habits and attitudes, it is advisable further to consider a few additional elements which are important in being liked and disliked. Don't develop a "poor me" attitude and desire too much attention and sympathy. A good substitute which will bring much better results is the studying and understanding of your partner's likes and dislikes, and judge yourself accordingly. Remember that because you like or dislike something, or an idea, it does not necessarily mean that it tallies with your partner's ideas. Be a student and discover these facts.

These are very important. Cater towards your partner's "pleasure principle" and don't step on his or her complexes. Develop a sense of confidence and independence with reliability. Don't try to get even with your partner. Finally, don't spy on your partner because if you do, you will finally see, or find out what you do not want to sec, or know, and you will suffer. If you do not discover negative findings, you may misinterpret certain situations. This is just as bad. Don't look for faults and don't be suspicious. Let your partner be convinced that you are looking for good points and qualities and these you will find. If you are suspicious and have a negative attitude, you will find trouble with the best partner. The question of love is very complex and the abilities and degrees of love vary directly in proportion to the personality, character, and understanding of the individuals concerned, and inversely, with the neurotic index. The permanency of love is more dependent on the abilities of intellectual transferences than on emotional transferences. Both emotional and intellectual transferences are involved and when the emotional transference alone exists, love is only of short duration. When the intellectual transference is added strongly to emotional transference, then love is made into a more permanent entity.

XXIII
Concluding Suggestions

A kiss, as it is practiced in America, is a form of affection and greeting between parents and children, husband and wife, sweethearts, relatives and friends. It is also used in court and in church to denote respect, piety, reverence, sincerity and honesty, as well as poetry.

Touching is the mother of the senses and kissing is related to the tactile (touch) sense. Though savages and primitive or other less civilized peoples, may either use the nose or other means symbolizing our labial kissing, European and American countries (particularly women) resort quite profusely to labial kissing, if not on the cheek, neck or hand, then more often on the lips directly. Though there are other specialized forms of kissing, no doubt the labial kiss predominates. Mothers, however, frequently kiss their babies, not only on their lips, but even their feet, etc. This, no doubt, represents love, affection and protection.

The mouth and lips are agents related to the satisfaction of hunger and love. It is quite evident that the meeting of two pairs of lips should connote love, trust, affection, tenderness, admiration, and that it is the present civilized method of proving endearment and closeness. When the mother kisses the child's aching or injured foot or hand, then crying ceases, because healing is supposed to have taken place through such behavior. Why does the infant respond so readily? why did the sick savage believe that he could be cured by the evil being sucked out of him through the mouth of another person?

Why do marriageable couples question the existence of

love if kissing is omitted? Why is a peck not considered a kiss or a sign of love? A peck does not show sufficient confidence, trust, emotions and feelings. A prolonged kiss indicates passion, but not necessarily the other desirable elements.

People seeing movies identify themselves with certain actors and actresses. This means that the spectators feel as the hero and heroine. If the actors are disappointed, or if they are rewarded, or whatever befalls them, immediately befalls the audience. Otherwise there is no interest and the picture is a flop. If the kiss is a peck, the audience does not get a sufficient chance to identify itself and receive the properly developed emotions. If the kiss is excessively prolonged, then the audience becomes fatigued, discovers that the audience is the audience, and that the individual or audience is not the actor or actors, and hence disappointment, loss of interest and there is failure to lose themselves in the imaginary world. The excessively short kiss means to many people a sort of duty, but coupled with indifference or fear and distrust. An excessively prolonged kiss also denotes, perhaps, a lack of trust, a lack of reason and unnecessary exhibitionism, and perhaps may bring forth laughter which may cause insincerity, and may interfere with the interest and the "escaping the world" which the public is seeking. Movies, T.V. and shows are for escaping, forgetting, entertaining and very little for learning.

A kiss lasting one second by a split-second stop watch is a usual home kiss and brings forth too little emotion on the part of an audience. A kiss lasting three seconds is usually longer than the ordinary home kiss, but it would give a movie audience sufficient time to recognize it with feeling. Let us say, a kiss lasting five or more seconds would cause uneasiness, unnaturalness, jealousy, and would interfere with interest. The best time is three to four seconds to create the best interest for movie fans.

Clinch scenes are helpful because they intensify the feelings and emotions of the actors and the audience. They add more reality and truthfulness to the imagination. The duration of the embrace has a similar meaning to that of kissing, but not to the same degree. The embrace may last twice as long and not be boring.

Olga Netherson and Mrs. Leslie Carter caused a sensation with their impassioned kisses, because they were properly timed, neither too long nor too short, and executed with a great feeling of emotion. Since all the correlating muscular activities were intensified and resonated and re-echoed the genuineness of these kisses, the audience became identified and was held spellbound, and consequently did not have time to doubt the reality of it. It was not a play, but REALITY. The identification was conscious and subconscious. As soon as the situation was made conscious, identification ceased, the imaginary word disappeared, and the poor individuals again had to face their cold, hard-boiled reality.

Human emotions are identically the same today as they were yesterday, but there are different methods of approach and ways of appeal. Human emotions and nature never change but the controls may vary.

The same psychological principles to be used in getting along with people should be applied to lovers in dealing with each other. In fact, since they are together so much, it is more important to exercise good psychology and good ethics. It is very essential to be tolerant, honest, tactful, and be very watchful and careful in controlling prejudices, jealousies and envy. Above all, there must be intellectual honesty, with no sarcasm, and quarrels must be prevented. Both should be resourceful with ideas, helpfulness, and strive for accomplishments. The possession and exercising of good personality traits, generally and specifically, are important.

It must not be taken for granted that everything is understood and tolerated between the two people. "Thank you," "Good-morning," and repetitions of love in words and gestures, are essential. The use of slang and derogatory and discouraging remarks should be avoided. The clinging to ideals is important. There should be no exaggerations, boasting, or fault-finding. Good substitutions are praise, flattery, and the expounding of the better qualities noticed in each other. There is certainly no room for peculiar emotions, anger and loudness. Voice modulation is so important, even when discussing irrelevant current events! Self-pity and excessive self-esteem create as many difficulties as do pettiness and dishonesty.

One should keep the body (externally and internally) clean, clothes, belongings and surroundings neat and presentable. Posture, gait, and smiling expressions are very helpful. Pettiness with money or using spendthrift tactics should be discouraged. The cultivation of any escape mechanism, such as too much drinking, too much religion, too much eating and smoking, excessive sleeping, indulging in hobbies to excess, are bound to lead to serious difficulties. The manifestations of inferiorities such as inactivities, shyness, the avoiding of certain people and activities, touchiness, irritability, boasting, and the various forms of shyness and withdrawing should all be eliminated or curtailed whenever possible. Substitute enthusiasm and courage, and admit mistakes if confronted with them, but understand the mechanism of these mistakes and strive to avoid them in the future. Be helpful, courageous, sympathetic, understanding, and see that you are an intellectual, honest, moldable and kind, simple human being.

Finally, honor and respect your mate, his or her parents, friends and associates, or at least, never belittle or hurt them. At the same time do not become too intimate with them for this will lead to disrespect or argument. "Familiarity breeds contempt."

Encourage and praise your partner and be consistent about it. This means that you should not encourage one day and discourage the next. In general, assume an optimistic attitude.

Though it is advisable to have a hobby yourself and to encourage your mate with a hobby, be careful that they are not conflicting hobbies or that they may result in competition.

Whatever you do, avoid suspicion on your part and on the part of your partner and friends, if possible.

Do not permit relatives, friends, or others to capture your interest which may cause a rift between your partner and yourself.

Don't over-buy clothing or other merchandise for yourself and preach economy for your partner, or permit your partner to violate the same.

Do not show excessive interests or over-praise your partner's sex.

Don't tease your partner or those associated with your partner.

If you want to joke with your partner, be sure it is in the form of encouragement and praise rather than castigation and belittling.

Carry out your promises if you can without too much sacrifice, yet don't hold your partner accountable for promises if they are too difficult to carry out, or unreasonable under new circumstances; nor should you throw up to your partner past omissions or mistakes. Forgive gracefully, heartily and do not carry grudges or pout. Try to understand the motivation for behavior in yourself and in your partner (consciously and unconsciously), then endeavor to explain it to yourself and to your partner if it does not cause too much resentment. Understand yourself first and then your partner.

XXIV

Questions for Study and Answer

In order to be a good lover or a good husband or wife, there must be a certain understanding. At times misunderstanding, erroneous ideas, complexes, certain selfishness, and defective judgment cause love to dwindle or become impossible.

The following are some questions which should be kept in mind, asked, understood, and properly answered by the reader. You can easily write a most interesting book answering these 100 questions. Everyone will flunk some of these questions.

1. Is your love peculiarly or partially selfish and to what degree?
2. Are you willing and anxious to sacrifice for the other party and to what degree?
3. Do you look for faults or for the good points in yourself as well as in your partner?
4. Do you carry grudges and pout?
5. Do you want to forget, or recall, past mistakes, errors and violations in yourself and in your partner?
6. Do you hold it against your partner because of what he said or did in the past, and how far do you carry this attitude?
7. In case of arguments with relatives or friends, do you argue with your partner or against him?
8. Do you like to see relatives and friends "show up" your partner?

9. Do you think, or make, the statement: "How in the world did you get along before you met me"?
10. Do you look forward to doing things in common?
11. Are you anxious to leave your work or office to come home, or do you find various reasons for either coming late or not at all?
12. In the presence of company, do you spend most of your time and attention with your partner or with your company?
13. If your parents or hers are present do you ignore them?
14. Do you feel that you understand your partner or do you substitute a feeling of mystery?
15. Do you try to "show up" or beat your partner in games, debates or in other competitive activities?
16. Do you envy others and compare your partner unfavorably with them?
17. Do you take your partner's hand, or like your hand to be held, while attending the movies?
18. Do you consult your partner before accepting invitations for entertainment and socials?
19. Do you like to correct your partner and enjoy finding reasons for such corrections?
20. Do you state that you regret being married or feel abnormally obligated to your partner?
21. Do you like to reminisce about your courtship and pleasant past experiences?
22. Do you like to keep in view recent photographs of your partner?
23. Are you very sensitive, or indifferent to the remarks of your partner?
24. Do you like to spare your partner's feelings?
25. Are you a frequent fault-finder?
26. Do you prefer spending time with your partner or with others?
27. Are you interested in the same literature, music, art, movies and other pleasures, entertainment and distractions as your partner?

28. Do you belittle each other because of your likes or dislikes?

29. Do you exchange gifts?

30. Are you interested in each other's clothing?

31. Do you become impatient when seeing your partner doing housework or other duties in a "slip-shod" or inefficient manner?

32. Do you like to tell your partner that you can do things better than he?

33. Are you late in meeting your partner?

34. Do you find fault with your partner's friends or relatives?

35. Is it often necessary to repeat questions to your partner?

36. Do you like to burden your partner with your problems, or do you prefer to consult with others first?

37. Do you mind exposing yourself or being ill-clad before your partner?

38. Are you bored paying special attention to your partner's special friends or relatives?

39. Do you feel ill at ease when your partner is uncomfortable?

40. Do you try to cater to your partner's interests?

41. Do you frequently try to show your good points to your partner, or do you let him find them himself?

42. Do you recall your partner's past mistakes, or do you belittle or forget them?

43. Do you criticize your partner's family unjustly?

44. Do you criticize your partner in front of your children or others?

45. Do you feel humiliated if you have to ask your partner for advice?

46. Can you detect easily when your partner is worried?

47. If your partner is tired or bored at a party, do

you suggest that both leave, or do you prefer that you remain a little longer?

48. Do you think your partner more attractive when silent, or when active and talking?

49. Do you think your friends were as good as, or better than, your partner's?

50. Do you think you could have found a better partner and hence regret your attachment?

51. Do you honestly believe yourself wise or foolish for your attachment?

52. Do you feel bored or resentful when you are consulted by your partner on matters whether new or old?

53. Are you happy or bored to pick presents for your partner?

54. Do you think your partner a spendthrift, inconsiderate, a poor or improper provider? Is it necessary to find an excuse to give your partner a present or to have an outing?

55. Do you prefer to prepare or buy the foods which your partner likes, and if so do you grumble about it?

56. Do you open your partner's mail voluntarily or involuntarily?

57. Do you respect your partner's clubs, societies and organizations?

58. Do you feel safe with your partner's affections?

59. Do you relish telling your partner your troubles, postpone it, or feel mixed up about such things?

60. Would you prefer your son or daughter to be like your partner, or different?

61. Do you think you or your partner can stand improvement?

62. Do you insist that certain duties must be performed by your partner or are you willing to cooperate and share the responsibilities?

63. Do you buy or help in purchasing your partner's clothes?

64. Do you prefer visiting with your partner or others?

65. In the presence of friends or relatives, would you prefer to make a good impression on your partner or on them?

66. Are you interested in your partner's relatives because of themselves or because they are relatives?

67. Do you agree with everything your partner says and does and, if not, do you reason it out between yourselves, ask for arbitration, have a quarrel, or leave the question unanswered and problems unsolved, or do you forceably handle the question your own way?

68. Do you like to see your partner make progress, or are you indifferent, or do you resent it?

69. Would you rather impress your partner, your parents, relatives, or others?

70. Do you dress to please yourself, your partner, or others?

71. Do you love your partner for your own welfare, his, or others?

72. Do you act happy with your partner to impress yourself, your partner, or others, or because you are happy?

73. Do you study how to improve your love-making, or are you satisfied with your present abilities?

74. Do you feel insecure with your partner's affections when alone, or in the presence of others, or under certain circumstances?

75. Do you try to impress your partner as to your superior or inferior qualities?

76. Would you rather see yourself or your partner improve?

77. If others praise your partner what do you think of the person doing so, or are you sceptical?

78. If others belittle your partner, are you influenced?

79. Would you prefer someone to praise you and

belittle your partner, or to belittle you and praise your partner?

80. As time goes on, does love grow, remain stationary, or recede?

81. Do you believe in love, and what is your attitude towards it?

82. Would you desire to effect an attachment or marriage to your ex-partner if you had your chances all over again?

83. Do you believe your family superior to your partner's?

84. Do you think of your partner when away from home or at work?

85. Are you thoroughly satisfied with your partner and prefer no changes, or do you desire changes in the person but you do not want to cause ill feelings?

86. Are you anxiously waiting to see your partner after being away for some hours?

87. Would you prefer to substitute yourself for pain and illness to spare your partner?

88. In case your partner were ill and wanted to see you, would you risk contagion and infection even against medical advice?

89. In case of aging would you prefer your partner to age more rapidly, or more slowly than yourself?

90. Do you believe in your partner's intuitive or reasoning abilities?

91. Are you attached to your partner largely because of frequent associations, or more so because of your partner's convinced qualities?

92. Do you consider your partner's best qualities to be physical, mental, social, or would you rather not analyze them?

93. Are you afraid to study your partner's good and weak points?

94. Have you made a study of your partner's family history, infancy, childhood, and adulthood; or are you uninterested?

95. Is your partner a detriment, or an asset, socially, mentally, physically and emotionally?

96. Do you feel at ease in talking about your partner's and your own strong and weak points without being emotional or antagonistic?

97. Do you feel peculiar about religious and political questions with respect to your partner, or do you think it makes no difference at all, or would you prefer that both of your opinions would coincide?

98. To what degree do you think your partner would sacrifice for you and you for him, regardless of knowing each other's degrees of sacrificing abilities?

99. Did you ever reflect how much you can do to make your partner happy?

100. Would you leave your partner if you were convinced that you are the cause of his unhappiness?